Seal it
with a *kiss*

D1602661

Seal it with a *kiss*

Tips, Tricks, and Techniques for Delivering the Knockout Kiss

Violet Blue

VIVA
EDITIONS

Published in the United States by Cleis Press Inc.,
P.O. Box 14697, San Francisco, California 94114.

Printed in the United States.
Cover design: Scott Idleman
Cover photograph: Davies and Starr
Text design and illustrations: Frank Wiedemann
Cleis Press logo art: Juana Alicia
First Edition.

10 9 8 7 6 5 4 3 2 1

ISBN: 978-1-57344-385-2

Library of Congress Cataloging-in-Publication Data

Blue, Violet.
Seal it with a kiss : tips, tricks, and secrets for delivering a knockout kiss / by Violet Blue. -- 1st ed.
    p. cm.
ISBN 978-1-57344-385-2 (trade paper : alk. paper)
1. Kissing. I. Title.

GT2640.B59 2010
394--dc22

                                        2009040954

CONTENTS

Introduction:

THE PERFECT KISS

A great kiss is like watching the ball drop in Times Square on New Year's Eve. There's the countdown to contact, the moment when your heart flutters from your stomach to your chest, and then—the kiss. You hear the noisemakers, people cheering, horns honking, confetti flies through the air, and you're caught in a vivid moment in time. Your heart warms (or ignites like a fuse). Your perspective changes, your senses sharpen, colors become more vivid, and you just know your brights will come out brighter than ever before. At least, that's what it feels like when the right pairs of lips come together in all the right ways.

Kisses like this are rare—but they don't have to be. Unfortunately, our lips didn't come with an owner's manual to tell us how to deliver smooches that stop traffic, start five-alarm fires, and warp the time–space continuum. Most of us have to figure that out by trial and error, and believe me, it isn't pretty. It messes up your lipstick, screws with your confidence, and you wind up pecking a lot of awful kissers. If only we could spot the lousy kissers, fix the ones we like, and if we just had ninjalike kissing skills, we'd be the baddest girls on the block with puckers that make urban legends seem tame.

That's what this book is for. This is where you learn to kiss like a movie star and make the one you're kissing feel as if his favorite song just came on the radio every time your lips come together. Find out how to time a kiss perfectly, how to deliver and get a first kiss, and how to ask for kisses with and without words. Learn how to know when someone wants to kiss you and what to do if the person you like turns out to be a bad kisser. Solve problems like stubble rash, and what happens when your kiss doesn't turn out the way you'd planned. Discover all the kissing do's and don'ts, and find out all the things you should never do when you kiss someone.

There are oodles of techniques in these pages to help you come up with—and perfect—your very own style for each lucky someone you kiss, no matter if you're a novice kisser or a make-out queen. Sex up your mouth and make it irresistibly kissable, then supercharge your kisses with advanced tricks, fun games, and tasty treats. Oh, and if you color your pucker, find out how to keep your lipstick perfect, no matter how hot and heavy (or wet and messy) your kissing session gets.

Don't stop with the lips—know your kissee's hot spots and get the skinny on how and where to kiss parts of the body that'll make them melt. Learn how to French-kiss like an angel (or a naughty devil) and all the different types of kisses and when to use them. Best of all, learn everything you need to make your first kiss with that special someone absolutely perfect and unforgettable.

Kissing is about chemistry—sometimes a kiss can be the moment we realize we're falling in love. The kind of connection experienced with a kiss can rock you to the core. But it doesn't have to be with someone you love—a kiss can be one of the most lighthearted ways of sharing intimacy with another person.

You can kiss as a sport, in a kissing booth for charity, or you can kiss someone just to find out if they are more interesting than you thought—all without commitment to either pair of lips involved. Or, if you choose, kissing can be the most intimate thing you share only with someone you love. But no matter how you kiss, or whom you kiss, you should always make it a doozy.

I hope you have as much fun putting this book into practice as I did doing the research for it.

Smooches,
Violet Blue
San Francisco

Chapter 1

THE SECRET SOCIETY
OF KISSING ARTISTS

The average woman spends two weeks of her life kissing—but what girl wants to be average? Two weeks of smooches just won't do—especially when you want to be the kind of kisser who has them coming back for seconds. And thirds. Maybe an all-you-can-kiss make-out buffet. With the secrets, tips, techniques, and detailed steps to becoming a master kisser in this book, you'll be more than the average player: you'll be at the top of the kissing game.

Kissing is one of the most sensual of all the acts of flirting, foreplay, seduction, and sex we can enjoy. In a kiss, you use all of your senses—and his too. You feel a kiss with your body, your heart, and your mind. You can communicate desire, urgency, caring—anything you want, because what you're feeling when you kiss someone can be channeled right through you like an electric charge. The greatest kissers know a variety of techniques that can be applied to a range of situations, tricks to make their kisses unforgettable, strategies to seduce even the shyest pair of lips, and how to jump-start that erotic spark with a first (or second, or third) kiss.

The sensual kisser has a lot more going on than a pair of kissable lips—though I'll tell you all about making your lips silky smooth and utterly irresistible in a bit. A truly sensual kisser is a girl who feels confident and sexy from within, no matter whether she happens to think she looks "perfect" at the moment, and a great kisser stays in touch with all of her senses—before kissing even begins. It's like flipping a light switch: when you know a kiss is about to happen, all of your senses sharpen. And once the kiss starts, everything goes into overdrive as you drink in the taste, the smell, the touch, the sound, the feelings. And the person on the receiving end is hooked.

What's in a Kiss?

Kissing is a single act that can convey a wide variety of intentions. For instance, one type of kiss, a light, affectionate peck, is a message of tenderness—it can be nonsexual, or a loving reminder. On the other hand, a first romantic kiss, built up to with nervousness and desire, might begin with the softest touch and pull you together like a red-hot magnet. A kiss between lovers is the spark that ignites passions into a blazing fire that may consume you both in a delicious make-out session. This kind of kiss can be more powerful than the need to eat when you're famished. Sometimes the prelude to a kiss is the best part; other times it's only a teasing, playful beginning.

One kiss can change everything. It can make friends into so much more. A kiss is the moment when sex and science meet, when we know whether our chemistry matches our desire. A casual encounter might turn into a pivotal, life-changing moment, after which ordinary everyday situations with your friend become lustful encounters. Often, when we kiss someone for the first time, we know instantly whether or not we click with them sexually.

Kissing is also really good for you and good for everyone around you. The act of kissing makes you feel emotionally ecstatic—it stimulates the release of endorphins, natural opiates similar to the delirious rush we feel while running and when we fall in love. Prolonged sensual kissing releases the arousal hormone oxytocin, essential for orgasm. And it's good for our teeth, because the increased flow of saliva washes our teeth in a plaque-dispersing bath. Now, doesn't that sound sexy?

Most of all, kissing is fun. Welcome to the world of kissing bandits and superkissers, where you'll learn how to cast an unforgettable, seductive spell with your lips. You'll join the legions of women who can melt a man like butter with a kiss, are always the first ones picked for the kissing booth, and can easily become rulers of small countries with their ability to deliver the perfect kiss anywhere, anytime.

The tips in this guide will make your past experiences with kissing seem like amateur night, and already-great kissers will find more secret kissing weapons, tips, and tricks to fortify their arsenal of techniques. Here you'll discover can't-fail techniques for ramping up your sensuality, the keys to perfect first kisses, the fine points of timing a kiss, oodles of techniques and surprises, and how to make an innocent kiss turn into a lustful session of tonsil hockey.

You don't need to be a man-eater or a villainous vixen to deliver the most wicked smooches—though all skill levels are encouraged to apply. Perhaps you're tired of being a one-date wonder or feel that you've missed far too many kissing opportunities. Or maybe you're a would-be kissing virtuoso, coiled up and ready to spring. Maybe you'd just like to know when and where different types of kisses are appropriate, how to be a better kisser, how to become a more magnetic kisser, or you want to learn new kissing techniques to make your sweetie give you—and your kissable lips—a double-take. This guide gives you concrete tools to nurture your kissing prowess, useful for a lifetime of being a first-rate, unforgettable kisser.

Kissing Kung Fu: Be at One with the Elements

Kissing begins with a pair of lips and a tongue. Pretty basic stuff. But a delivering a *great* kiss isn't just "tab A into slot B." What makes the perfect kiss has to do with so much more than a pair of squishy body parts getting mashed together. Desire, passion, tenderness, comfort, lust, yearning for connection, the urge to capitalize on a "perfect moment," and more, all drive us to kiss. Add to that the elements of atmosphere and timing, and you've got a whole slew of ingredients that can make whatever you've got cooking sweet or sour. Examine what elements make a kiss perfect—or pitiful.

❀Timing is everything. In the movies, when the hero leans over to kiss the leading lady, the timing is always perfect— the sun is setting, both kissers feel amorous, birds are chirping, and all is good in the world. In real life, you may have the same experience, or your birds may actually be car alarms, passersby may be wishing you weren't doing that in public, you might be unexpectedly queasy from cocktails or nerves, or a meteor could be on a collision course with Earth. Worse, a kiss when you don't want one isn't a kiss at all—it's a drag. A great kiss happens right when it is supposed to, while an ill-timed kiss can ruin everything and practically peel the paint off the walls.

❀You know this: it's got to be the right pair of lips heading for your face, or all bets are off. Is the kisser your fantasy man, or is he a drooling fool from Planet Lame? If your date is Mr. Delicious, then your goodnight kiss has got to be a doozy. But if you don't click with the person planting one on you, then you've got a scary mouthful of Mr. Yikes.

❀Location, location, location. A wispy kiss on a mountaintop might be your idea of romantic perfection, or a sloppy session on the floor behind your roommate's couch could be at the top of your list. But if you smooch in a location that isn't right for one of you (say, in a public space that makes you or him feel exposed or otherwise uncomfortable), the kiss will bomb like an attempt to make *Titanic* into a romantic comedy.

❀It's got to feel good physically, too. Is the kiss a perfect union of lips and tongue, dancing in tandem to create an emotional connection? Does it make an electric spark that sends buzzy, yummy jolts of lust straight to your nethers? Or is it a smooshy mush of slippery lips and tongues that slither like slimy, wilted slugs? If a kiss feels good, you're on top of the world, but if a kiss feels yucky, too wet, or just plain wrong, it's a dud.

❀How a kiss makes you feel can make or break a mood, and it's one of the more sublime elements to consider. The feelings behind a kiss are like a supporting actor who completes the character and identity of the leading lady. Is the kiss an emotional gesture that comes from the heart, or a raw animal thing that comes from the groin? And how do you gauge the feelings of the person kissing you? Does he feel the same way? There are ways to tell how your kissee is feeling, and when his signs and signals are green for "go" when your own engine is revved, then you're kissing in sync.

❧Believe it or not, the motive for your kiss is communicated through your lips at the moment of contact, and it instantly sets the tone for any given smooch. Perhaps you are a devious femme out on a kissing conquest, taking what you want from the lips of hapless mortals. Lust, kiss, and conquer. Maybe you're a shy and lovely thing, ready to smooch, cuddle with a few sweet fairy kisses, and nuzzle with someone you adore. Or you might be both, depending on which way the kissing goes. A great kiss is made of many elements and can take you down different paths. Think about what you want out of it before you pucker up, buttercup.

❧Technique is the foundation of your kissing style. And the technique you use depends on all of the factors and goals mentioned above—or you might just be out for fun, freestyling. Either way, your technique says it all, and you'll enjoy kissing, and the reaction your kisses get, when you have an arsenal of styles in your naughty bag of kissing tricks.

Kiss Me Deadly, Darling: A Quiz

Kissing might be the one thing you know makes 'em swoon with desire, or kisses might be just part of your playful bag of down-and-dirty flirty tricks. What kind of kisser are you?

When I kiss someone for the first time, I never:
A. make the first move.

B. move my body too close to his.

C. remove all of my clothes, just most of them.

D. set him free, no matter how much he begs.

The perfect movie kiss was:
A. Rhett Butler and Scarlett O'Hara in *Gone with the Wind*.

B. Kirsten Dunst and Tobey Maguire in *Spider-Man*.

C. the vampiresses and any poor mortal man in *The Brides of Dracula*.

D. the elevator scene in *Fatal Attraction*.

I always make the first move kissing:
A. never!

B. when I know it's absolutely safe to do so.

C. before the cocktails wear off.

D. when he's trapped like a wild animal.

When kissing on the first date, I never:
A. use tongue.
B. let it get too steamy.
C. let underwear get in the way.
D. let my emotions get in the way of my evil plans to destroy my enemies.

Your philosophy about kissing is:
A. Kissing is fun but should be shared with someone special.
B. Good kissers are hard to find.
C. They are all my playthings and victims, every last one of them.
D. Never let them up for air.

I get ready for a kiss by:
A. keeping my lips and mouth in beautiful shape.
B. thinking about what kinds of kisses my kissee might really enjoy.
C. swishing with the last gulp of my beer, and off I go!
D. surveying bedpost notches and emitting a fearful cackle while overwhelmed with evil satisfaction.

Kissing someone is how I tell:
A. what kind of lover he might be.
B. if we really click.
C. how much his girlfriend means to him.
D. how long it will take to convert such a meddlesome hero to the Dark Side.

Your scariest nightmare about kissing contains:

A. someone who just wants to get in my panties.
B. waiting to kiss someone and then finding out they're a terrible kisser.
C. a man who kisses like he's cleaning a fish tank with his tongue.
D. kittens, romantic sunsets, happy endings, not becoming absolute ruler of the universe, fluffy bunnies, all that is good and nice.

My surefire red-hot kissing technique is:

A. Keep my lips closed together and my hands to myself.
B. Follow his lead with tongue and touching, but take over when things get hot.
C. Try to swallow his entire face, lick everywhere from the neck up, insert entire tongue into his throat.
D. Unhinge jaw, swallow entire man.

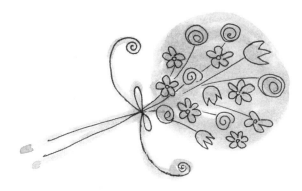

If you answered mostly "A," you are Sweet Lips.

You're sweet as sugar, and your kisses are, too—and the person you're kissing knows that your cute little pucker and slightly naughty smile screams "sexy!" Your kissing power lies in your ability to seduce and tease longingly, making your make-out sessions dreamy and lasting, like an all-day lollipop. Attractive lips and a subtle style make your kisses unforgettable; learn a few dirtier tricks and the electric shocks from your tongue will bring them to their knees.

Your kissing mantra is: "Melts in your mouth, not in your hands."

If you answered mostly "B," you are Power Puss.

Mack Daddy, meet Mack Mama. Your lips like to boogie, but before they hit the dance floor, they like to taste, road-test, and compare. You like to sample the goods before committing to a date, or to a make-out session, or even just to see what the local boys taste like—you like to test the water before you jump in. You're a Power Kisser, through and through. Hone your skills, and they'll name a lipstick shade after you.

Your kissing mantra is: "Victoria's got nothing on my Secret."

If you answered mostly "C," you are Hot Lips.
Your kisses are like a wildfire, and if you have your way, it'll take a station full of firefighters to control the blaze. You're a femme fatale kisser who never misses, and you're just as happy to give your dates a taste of your tongue and strut away leaving them swooning. Your kisses are the strong, silent type that come and go like a storm, and with a little polishing from the tips in these pages, your lips will be legendary—and lethal.

Your kissing mantra is: "Hello—my name is Your Addiction."

If you answered mostly "D," you are Pure Delicious Poison.
Remember supervillainess Poison Ivy? She's just a shrub compared to you. A kiss from you, blown on the wind, has been known to wilt flowers and make babies cry miles away. Your plan to conquer the universe one man at a time is unstoppable, and kisses are just the hors d'oeuvres of delicious conquest to you. It's hard to go wrong when you're already so bad, but keeping your kisser in picture-perfect shape and building an arsenal of smooching styles will keep your seductive powers at their most fearful.

Your kissing mantra is: "I'm so hungry I could eat—anyone I want."

Chapter 2:

MAKE IT HAPPEN: GET THAT KISS ANYWHERE, ANYPLACE, ANYTIME

The awkward moment: It's happened to you. At the end of the evening, you walk to your car to say good-bye and— your stomach flips. Your heart flutters. Your brain explodes. He looks at you, and you feel an electric charge in the air. Then maybe, just maybe... You get in your car and drive away fast like a frightened little bunny. Let's hope *not*.

An attack of shyness happens to all kissers, from beginners to the suavest and most experienced lip-lockers. The awkward moment of the first kiss can turn even the coolest cucumber into the biggest spaz. Some people love the moment before the first kiss, the excitement, the terror— the moment you've both been waiting for when attraction leads to intimate contact. Others dread it and will squirm every which way to avoid having to make a move. The anticipation is delicious, delightful, agonizing—thrilling. It means you're *alive*.

Sometimes the anticipation of your first kiss is the best part. Taking your time to build up the attraction and excitement makes your first kiss that much more unforgettable— and wonderfully, passionately explosive. When you're both so eager to kiss that you just can't stand it anymore, your attraction to each other becomes powerful, magnetic—and when the kiss finally happens, you see the stars. Do you have the self-restraint to wait until you just can't take it anymore?

Waiting for the first kiss can be like a tightrope walk. You must proceed very carefully so as not to rush things, on one hand, or send signals that you're not as interested as you really are, on the other. It's a little stressful, but it's much easier when you know how to read your partner's signs and how to send the right message to get what you want.

Waiting Is the Hardest Part

You might not kiss on the first date for a number of reasons—and he might actually be the one who wants to wait. If he asks to wait a few dates for a first kiss, honor his request with grace and a smile, and relish the thought that anticipation is building up mutually. Don't worry about his reasons; they're probably good ones, whatever they are. Don't second-guess, either. He might simply just be shy! Feed the fires by being casually flirty in subtle physical ways—a touch on the wrist, or standing or sitting a bit too close. And if you've both agreed to wait for that fiery first kiss, you can cuddle, hug, and breathe on each other's lips, only inches away from each other.

Some of you might want to wait a bit for the first kiss to see if there is chemistry between you. Or, like any femme fatale worth the notches on her bedpost, you might want to make him wait simply to enjoy watching him squirm in erotic torment, willing to do anything for your first kiss. Clever smoochers might want to camouflage ill health, such as a flu or allergies, by asking to delay the first kiss for a few dates, until you're feeling better or know the potential kissee a bit better. Maybe you have already rushed to first base, or second or third, too fast for your own liking, and you want to take a bit more time to smell the roses.

It's perfectly fine to tell him you want to wait a bit before your first kiss, or to wait until the third date. Reassure him that it's not personal (he might feel insulted or insecure) and explain that you just don't want to rush a good thing. Tell him that you'll make the first move when you're ready to enjoy it completely.

If you prefer not to announce your intentions, be sure to give him other signals that you're interested; otherwise he'll think you don't want him at all. Yikes! Flirt with him, lightly touch his arm or hands now and then, brush against him a little when you walk down the sidewalk, make plenty of eye contact, smile a lot, and don't be afraid to stand or sit closer than a regular friend might.

If he moves in for a kiss and you're still not ready, place your hands flat on the front of his shoulders to gently, firmly stop him. Stay close, smile, and sweetly say, "I'm not ready yet. But I will be soon. It means a lot that you're cool with that." You can softly kiss his cheek instead. Some guys might not understand why you want to wait for a kiss. They might protest, get upset, be pushy, demand reassurance, or argue. The rotten ones will insist. (This is okay if you know that you enjoy a little playful protest in your romantic relationships.) But the guys who are truly worth kissing will listen

17

and will want to understand your motives—and the really fun ones will want to draw out the anticipation and savor the first-kiss waiting game as much as you do.

Does He Really Want It?

Yes, hot pants, they all want you. But only give 'em a little nibble at a time. When sizing up your toy for a potential smooch, make sure he's really ready for the close-up by looking for physical clues that reveal his readiness. Some guys will make it fairly obvious that it's now or never by moving in for the kiss, but others will display unconscious physical signs to indicate readiness and kissability. And I'm not talking about what's happening in his trousers. It's especially essential to know what to look for with shy guys who want to be respectful of your kissing boundaries. Are you sending the green light? Often, they want to kiss us oh-so-badly, but they have no idea that we actually want them to kiss us! Also, it's tough to tell if someone wants to go beyond friendship or not, especially when your judgment is clouded by your own attraction to someone you realize is becoming more than just a friend.

It's up to you to figure out if he wants it or not. Does he call, text, IM, Tweet, or email you frequently? If you're out together on a date or just hanging out, remember that he could choose to be spending his in-person time with someone else. But he's with *you*. Put yourselves in a situation that would be an ideal time for a kiss, such as saying good-bye, and watch his body language closely for unconscious signs of attraction. Make sure you see two "kiss now" signals before you take the leap with your lips.

Just what are those signals? Prolonged and repeated eye contact is a sure sign of interest, and combined with close physical proximity is a sure signal of an impending kiss. If you catch him checking you out, bust him playfully with a smile that says "gotcha!" and flirt shamelessly, enjoying every moment. One careless glance from him isn't enough, but if there is a second look, stay tuned for more. When his second look lingers for a bit, consider this an engraved invitation: you've got him right where you want him. If the eye contact is fleeting and you can't tell if it's intentional or not, wait to see if it happens more than once and look for another physical clue just to be sure.

Here are a few clues to look for:

❀**Clue:** Look to the lips. When people are tense or uninterested, they keep their lips clamped together. But when someone finds you hot and wants a smooch, their lips will part slightly in an inviting gesture. Like, smiling! Licking the lips (not in a gross or creepy way!) or touching the lips with a finger can indicate high kissing interest.

❀**Clue:** Unconscious imitation is someone's way of showing that they'll follow your lead, including up to the moment of a kiss. Watch and see if he mirrors your body language—legs crossed or uncrossed, the position of his hands and arms, shoulders squared to face you directly, and of course, mirrored facial expressions such as eye contact, smiling, and moving in close.

❀**Clue:** Close physical proximity. Arms brushing when you walk, a slight touch on the arm or hand, orbiting your stance in crowded rooms, standing so your shoulders touch, being just a half step closer to you than he would to someone who's just a friend. Notice whether he's keeping an eye on where you are and where you're standing. Often, interested men will have conversations with others near you or (especially) right behind you. Another clue that precedes a kiss is for him to hold open a door for you in a way that intentionally has him leaning in close as you move past. This is a great opportunity for a smile—or a kiss.

How to Get Him to Kiss You

Of course, there's nothing wrong with the direct approach. Some people love nothing more than to have their partner simply ask for a kiss. Have you ever hoped for a kiss, not gone for it or even asked for one, and then not been kissed? I can predict how well that technique is working for you. A girl or guy who's a little bit (or a lot) aggressive when it comes to the sweet pastime of kissing gets what they want, and many women and men love a partner who isn't afraid to take control.

Ask for that kiss:

"May I have a kiss, please?"
"Kiss me!"
"You can kiss me now."
"I think you deserve a kiss for that."
"Aren't you forgetting something?"
"Can we kiss now?"
"Pucker up, buttercup."

Asking for it is only one option for getting him to put those sexy lips right where you want them: on you. You don't always have to ask with words; you can hypnotize him with a few super-sexy moves. Seriously. Even if you're the direct-approach kind of girl, words may not be appropriate for the scenario you find yourself in; you may have to be quiet for some reason, or asking for a smooch outright may simply not be your style. No problem. Whether you're shy or cunning, you have an arsenal of tricks to choose from.

How to Ask for a Kiss without Words
First, open up your body language so he can sense that you're receptive for him to put the moves on you. Or that you're even interested: you can convey a lot of interest just by the way you carry yourself. Pull your shoulders back and take a slow, deep breath, and imagine your shoulders opening wider, with the center of your chest pulling upward. Straighten up your posture and arch (curve) your lower back a bit. Sitting or standing, you can do all this within the space of a few breaths and no on will notice—except, subliminally, him. Pull your head up and back just slightly, as well.

Eye contact is the golden key for getting that kiss without actually asking for it out loud. Your kissing mind-control efforts are centered on what you do with your eyes, and if you stare at the ground (or anywhere but his eyes and lips), he'll think you're not interested. To get his attention, you can softly touch his arm, shoulder, or the back of a hand.

Did you take the "Kiss Me Deadly, Darling" test in chapter 1? Choose your techniques from the options below. Each of them is an excellent prelude to making the first move if you get tired of waiting and just want to plant one on him to see if he's worth it!

For Sweet Lips sweeties:

Make eye contact, smile, and incline your head close to his. If you're shy or nervous you can look away at intervals, but be sure to always return your eyes to his and smile softly as you make contact again.

For Power Puss playas:

Let your eyes linger for a relaxed breath. Make eye contact, and then break it to look at his lips, and then back to his eyes. Smile. A sexy, closed-mouth smile with the corners of your mouth is an erotic invitation—use this sweetly tricky smile to your advantage. Repeat as needed, and don't be afraid to maintain eye contact while blinking.

For Hot Lips and Poison Kiss divas:

Your lips are the most suggestive, sensual erogenous zone you've got—work it, girl, and get his attention focused right where it belongs. The instant you want that smooch, subliminally make him look at your lips to suggest kissing (and sex). Enjoy playing around with what touches your lips, how you touch them, and what slips between them. Bite your lower lip suggestively while smiling to tease and tempt. Rub your lips together softly and smile. Bite the end of your finger for a second—tilting your head down to do this is very flattering to your eyes and face. Touch your straw to your lips before you take a sip. Rub your lips lightly on the edge of a glass, as if you are doing it unconsciously. If you're not sure he is paying attention, direct his gaze to your lips with a pen, a finger, a straw, a snack, a lollipop, or a spoon. If you're feeling really bold, move your lips close to his without making contact while you talk, and linger for a breath or two to push it even further.

Making the First Move

The first kiss is often a make-or-break deal, where both of you find out if all this excitement is really what it's cracked up to be. If the object of your desire doesn't make the first move, getting up the courage to initiate the kiss is important, but equally crucial is how you kiss him the very first time. Your technique is everything here, because it communicates much more about you than words and gives him a direct indication of the passion that's got you all fired up.

It's debatable whether you should French-kiss (with your tongue) when you kiss someone the very first time. Certainly, at the moment of contact, your tongue should remain within your mouth—but how the kiss progresses past that point is a matter of assessing the direction and flow of the kiss. If you press lips and are overcome with passion and crazy desire, you'll find your tongues dancing within moments, seemingly without any permission from your brain. When that happens, you just have to go with it. And if your first kiss turns out to be the kind where he passionately grabs you and you both uncontrollably start dancing the tongue tango, no one will blame you for not following any first-kiss "rules."

But unless you're crawling all over each other like love weasels on a hot summer night, keep that tongue in check until you've kissed three or four times, or until you've been open-mouth kissing for several minutes.

First Kiss Do's and Don'ts:

Do smile a lot, even while kissing.

Do keep eye contact.

Do make sure you have nice breath.

Do remember to come up for air.

Do start slow.

Do begin with small movements of the lips, head, body, and hands.

If you make the first move, do pull back after the first kiss to gauge his or her response.

Do keep your lips soft and the muscles relaxed— not hard or tight.

Do keep your tongue in your mouth (see above).

Do linger for a moment after the kiss. Especially for a smile.

Do pay attention to where your noses are going and avoid a collision.

Don't approach the kiss with your mouth open.

Don't worry if you collide! Laugh and move in again slow.

Don't jam your tongue in his mouth.

Don't slobber!

Don't make yummy noises—yet.

Don't make overly loud kissing or "smacking" noises.

Don't let your hands wander.

Don't start off with bites or suction.

Don't rush—savor this moment, even if you're nervous.

Don't worry about what you look like.

Don't attempt this kiss if you're not feeling well.

Don't finish the kiss abruptly, even if you don't like it.

Don't forget to breathe!

Chapter 3:

YOUR MOUTH: HE'S GOTTA HAVE IT

When it comes to erotic hot spots on the human body, nothing beats our most visual and versatile sex organ, the mouth. With our mouth, uniquely controlled by hundreds of muscles, we can communicate intentions, ideas, and desires, and we can deliver kisses that make him feel like he's in Nirvana.

We forget how powerful our pretty little mouths are. Without a word, we can smile and flirt, we can warm up a room or a lover with peals of laughter, and most especially we can lick, bite, taste, smell, and literally inhale sex through our mouth. A sexy mouth suggests that one sensual opening can lead to another, elsewhere on the body, or in the heart and mind. Our lips suggest contours of genitalia, and a hint of wetness or the appearance of a tongue implies much more—sex itself.

And as owner of this highly sensitive and tactile sensory organ, we do love to put things in our mouth. You've no doubt heard the term *orally fixated* in polite company in reference to smoking cigarettes. Inevitably everyone within earshot gets a little tingle from the implications.

It is true that as a culture we're orally fixated, constantly looking for the next thing going into our mouth, and it's equally true that the right kind of oral stimulation can really turn us on. So maybe we're just a bunch of orally obsessed hedonists—so what? Soak up all the pleasure your lips, tongue, and mouth can afford you. Use it to its erotic maximum every chance you get, and see how your love life explodes.

Hot Lips

Cut to the chase, sexy. Recognize your mouth for the sex organ it is: treat it accordingly, and learn the many delightful things you can do with it before you even kiss. A healthy-looking mouth sends signals to potential partners on subtle levels. Make your entire mouth even sexier by giving it extra attention the next time you brush your teeth. Along with your lips, brush your tongue to make it look smoother and sexily pink, and be sure to brush the roof of your mouth— an oft-forgotten spot that, if ignored, can contribute to bad breath.

Lips are unabashedly sexual, and they cannot be hidden. So turn up the volume, already. Delight in your lips. They are the most expressive, sensual erogenous zone we've got—and they're right there on your face. When someone is interested in you, he'll look at your lips almost as much as your eyes. To subliminally suggest sex, you can slyly direct him to look at your lips throughout the communication, whether you're talking or not.

Deepen the color of your lips even just slightly and you'll draw erotic attention to this powerful visual erogenous zone. You don't need to wear lipstick, though sexy shades (or even a tinted moisturizer) go a long way to attract attention and magnetize your prey. Keep your lips exfoliated by rubbing them lightly with your toothbrush daily, or use your regular exfoliating scrub lightly on your lips each time you use it on your face. This will slough off any dead cells, keep away dry flat bits, and make your lips look supple and naturally healthy. Follow up with a moisturizing balm and a coat of something glossy for extra-sexy appeal.

Our lips swell during arousal, giving off a rosy flush that communicates passion and lust to our lovers on an animal level. Amp up the lip plump by drawing blood to them via daily exfoliation. Several companies now sell "lip plumping" glosses and lipsticks (most notably Lip Venom by Du Wop) that boost your lips slightly or smooth out the lip surface and fill in the cracks to make lips look larger.

If you feel your lips need more than a gloss or a tingly boost from lip plumpers, there are a number of multi-step lip care regimens you can employ to get your lips in ultra-pretty, kissable shape. Beyond using a high-quality moisturizer such as Nivea, Lancôme, Laura Mercier, or even Biotherm, a lip-beautifying routine might be just what the lip doctor ordered. The multi-step methodology typically includes exfoliation, extracting impurities (using a lip mask), smoothing, moisturizing, and promoting the production of collagen (to prevent aging and wrinkles where your lips meet facial skin). Brands include Serious Lip Treatment by MD Skincare, Eminence Lip Trio Kit, and Mary Kay's Satin Lips two-step process.

Talented Tongue

Unlike our lips, our tongue is a naughty, haughty, pink, wet, fleshy, unashamedly sexual body part—and therefore typically kept hidden. A muscle of many tactile talents, the tongue is a clever little package of muscles, glands, and sensitive nerves. Nerves lead from the tongue to the brain, which within an instant of contact sends sensations of touch, scent, and taste. The "flavor" of anything we put in our mouth is a complex combination of taste, smell, touch, texture or consistency, and temperature sensations.

Your lips, tongue, and mouth are controlled by hundreds of muscles that never rest as you smooch, smile, scowl, unconsciously clench your jaw, or suck on your tongue. This diligent network of muscles allow us to soften our lips, pull them apart, draw them closed to an O, and to point or lightly stroke with our tongue. You can lengthen your tongue, shorten it, or move it in a variety of directions while kissing, and your neck and jaw muscles work in tandem to give your tongue greater versatility. These muscles also make the insides of the mouth into a means of suction that can draw lemonade through a straw, or give a kiss an especially naughty twist when you lightly give his inquiring tongue a sucking tug. There are dozens of strokes, licks, and various combinations of suction that you'll want to incorporate into your oral arsenal.

Mouth Moves

These basic moves might sound silly at first, but try them a few times to get the hang of them. They'll be the basis for kissing techniques later in this book, and they'll get your mouth in shape, make you aware of your mouth's moves, and give you ideas for ramping up your personal kissing style. Try these at home when you're alone, even in front of a mirror if you want.

❀Pucker your lips. Hard and small, softer and wider, very soft and very wide (a half-smile).

❀Purse your lips. Like blowing a kiss: firm and short, soft and fluid, like Marilyn Monroe.

❀Point your tongue. Stick it out a little, then a lot.

❀Look in the mirror and soften your tongue. Extend it soft.

❀Sweep your tongue around your lips—pointed and hard, then flat and soft.

❀Suck on your sensitive little finger—a little, then a lot.

❀Kiss the palm of your hand softly, then more firmly; then see how it feels to mash your lips into it. Your palms are sensitive and perfect for practicing the sensations of kissing his lips, face, neck, and more.

❀On the back of your hand, practice tongue strokes and see how they might feel for your sweetie. Poke, lick, flatten your tongue and sweep, draw letters of the alphabet with the tip.

❀Make your lips into an O and suck on your palm. Apply suction to draw sensation to the area and then lightly rub your teeth across the sensitive spot.

The Wicked Kisser

Feeling naughty, darling? Draw them into your wicked web by making your whole aura into a seductive hot zone, with your kisses at the center of it. Before you learn to seduce someone else's senses with your super-sensual kisses, you'll need to get in touch with the sensuality and sexuality in your own body.

Not everyone feels she's hot all the time, and not everyone needs to be told how to feel sexy, but doing a few nice things for yourself can get you in the right head space for kissing. Then you can build a set of tools (a sensual checklist) to give you confidence and sexiness when you may not be feeling so hot, are feeling nervous, or really want to unleash every trick in the book on your unsuspecting target.

Sex Up Your Lips, and the Rest Will Follow

Touch

Splurge on a massage or spa treatment to get back in touch—literally—with your body. Let someone else do all the work while you relax and enjoy healing touch from a massage therapist. Or take a hot bath and treat yourself to some new lotions and potions—have a self-care beauty night. Create some private time to touch your own body the way you'd like a lover to, and let your fantasies run wild.

Sight

How you look affects how you feel. Purchase items or treatments that make you look polished, sexy, and hot. Get a manicure or pedicure, a facial, a haircut—go in for a wash-and-dry style, just for fun. Indulge in a new lip color or gloss, a new makeup color, or accessories for your ears, hair, and neck. Buy a new item of sexy, comfortable clothing, something relaxed but seductive—or put on an old favorite.

Smell

Aromatherapy really works to make us feel sexy, sensual, and at ease with ourselves. If you're the kind of person who wears a fragrance, then you've got it covered with your favorites, but you can also mix things up with a new scent, just for kicks. Those who prefer more subtle ways of scenting their skin should pick up a sexy-smelling new lotion—with a bit on the nape of the neck, your world smells instantly sexier. If your hair covers your ears, you can put a little scent in your hair, or use a yummy-smelling conditioner for when things get deliciously close.

Sound

Great music to kiss by is covered later in this book—right now you're going to focus on making yourself sound sweetly seductive. Becoming intimate, in the build-up to the moment of a kiss, means weaving a spell with everything about your mouth: every word you speak—even whispered—will have to be sexy and seductive. Make your voice one of your captivating charms, and learn how to modulate it effectively to the point of contact, and beyond.

Find your sexiest voice. Some people have a difficult time hearing their own voice and might find that trying a few voice exercises gives them a sexier and more resonant sound. Practice speaking not from your throat but from the center of your chest, and power the air from your stomach muscles. Stretch the muscles on your jaw, lips, and tongue to relax your face. Learn to speak softly by lowering your volume (loudness) and pitch (lower notes), but play with resonance.

Try a sentence in a low whisper, deeper than your normal voice. Then try it louder, still a bit deeper. Next, hum, keeping your mouth closed. Now speak the sentence in your low whisper, but with the same resonance as the hum. You'll use these different techniques to find the sexy voice that works best for you, and also to gauge volume over music, to match up with your kissing partner's volume, and turn it down as you move in for a kiss.

Taste

How you taste to your kissing partner is one thing (more about flavored kisses and other tricks in a bit), but how cultivated and sensual your tasting abilities are is another thing altogether. Wake up those taste buds! A delicious kiss can be like a long, delirious drink of water when you're thirsty, and you'll want to be able to drink in how your lover tastes to the fullest. Sharpen your sense of taste, and heighten your sexuality, by sampling food with aphrodisiac qualities.

Foods with sexual reputations cover a variety of sumptuous textures, perfect for getting you in the right kissing state of mind. Some classics: strawberries with chocolate sauce, a salad of quartered figs, shredded basil with drips of balsamic vinegar, warmed honey, avocados, vanilla bean (can be in ice cream), licorice, candied rose petals, and mango or papaya spears wrapped in mint leaves.

Chapter 4

KISSING: A FIELD GUIDE

First, let's see who's on the menu, and what he might taste like for a nibble. A field guide to identifying the different types of kissing animals in the smooching zoo can help you find the perfect fit. Will he kiss like a Rock Star, or make love with his lips like a Geek Boy? Learn the difference, see how they like their first kisses, and wow the kiss-target of your dreams into kissing bliss with the right techniques.

The Hunters and the Hunted

Rock Star

Appearance: Fashionably disheveled, trendy, and sexy.

Attitude: Ready to rock those lips harder than Judas Priest.

Ideal first kiss: Backstage, in the limo, in a trashed hotel room, or in an atmospheric alleyway.

Kissing don't: Rock stars are born to rock. Let the rocker make the first move.

Yuppie

Appearance: Wrinkle-free.

Attitude: Willing to fog up glasses and spill latte for the greater good of kissing.

Ideal first kiss: Tastes like Starbucks or California Zinfandel.

Kissing don't: Loves playfully aggressive kissers, hates overeager or domineering. Know the difference.

Art School Brat

Appearance: Thrift-store trendy; no spending limit on hairdo.

Attitude: While others kiss like lower beasts, to them kissing is an art.

Ideal first kiss: After completion of most recent master-piece, or off-hours in the studio.

Kissing don't: Too sensitive to make the first move, they'll give up and make a video blog if you wait for them to kiss you.

Marketing Executive

Appearance: Sinister, like a politician. Nice suits.

Attitude: There's a time for kissing and a time for world domination of my brand—er, work.

Ideal first kiss: Office, after hours.

Kissing don't: Never talk during kisses, unless it's dirty talk about corporate branding.

Supervillain

Appearance: Evil like the Marketing Executive but with more Spandex and a fluffy white cat.

Attitude: Hell-bent on destroying all that is good and nice.

Ideal first kiss: Secret lair, private island, castle, top of the Washington Monument after starting clock on doomsday device.

Kissing don't: Never smooch in front of the do-gooder enemies and heroes. It just doesn't look right.

Hero

Appearance: Proud, big chin, cape.

Attitude: Evil must be stopped, blah, blah, blah.

Ideal first kiss: Suspended over a pit of alligators right before escape, after saving you, or out of costume when you think he's someone else.

Kissing don't: This one's IQ plummets like a lead balloon with a kiss, so only kiss after danger has passed—unless you're the danger.

Gangster

Appearance: Changes by location; can be gold chains, a pimpin' ride, and baggy pants, or Italian suits and fedoras.

Attitude: Gimme some sugar, baby.

Ideal first kiss: After watching *Scarface*.

Kissing don't: Not during *The Sopranos* or in front of "the boys."

Romantic

Appearance: Bedroom eyes and mussy-touseled hair.

Attitude: Kissing is a beautiful thing shared between two people.

Ideal first kiss: Mountaintop, picturesque vista, picnic for two, movie theater.

Kissing don't: The first kiss has to be perfect with this one; don't rush it.

Man Slut

Appearance: Partly undressed; gold chains or cutoff jean shorts a bonus.

Attitude: Who's going home with the king tonight? Or, who's next?

Ideal first kiss: As often as possible.

Kissing don't: Don't expect that quantity means quality—this one's been around the block and back (and forth, and back) because he's not one for polishing his technique. But for quickie smooches, it's always a sure thing with a slutmuffin.

Male Model

Appearance: A little too perfectly done, and all eyes are on him.

Attitude: Kissing me will make you look like a star.

Ideal first kiss: Only in flattering lighting, no tongues, and definitely no hickeys. If anyone sees it, it will have to look perfect.

Kissing don't: Under no circumstances do you mess up the hair! The hair is sacred.

Rough Trade

Appearance: Sexy stubble, jeans, work boots, and a dimpled smile.

Attitude: I work hard, and I kiss like I mean it.

Ideal first kiss: At the end of a great date, with him taking the lead.

Kissing don't: Unless you smell like you ate too many cocktail weenies, it's tough to go wrong with this easy-going smoocher.

Geek Boy

Appearance: Clothes don't fit, soft and sweaty hands, pale skin, blinded by sunlight, brain like a supercomputer.

Attitude: Afraid of girls but can't stay away. They tend to be inexperienced kissers, yet sincere. Once uncorked, their sensual powers are frightening.

Ideal first kiss: Um, any.

Kissing don't: Quick movements will frighten them, but soft kisses will soothe.

Anyone can kiss. But a kisser who knows her moves is a force to reckon with. A scandalous agenda helps, but becoming familiar with the full range of kisses—what they mean, how to use them, and when to bring out the big guns—makes them roll over and bark the minute your lips enter the room. With all the right moves, that Goodnight Kiss will be a doozy, you'll know how to deliver the prefect Taste of What's to Come, and how to identify and avoid the horrifying Fish Tank Kiss.

Types of Kisses

Some kisses are standard—the Goodnight Kiss is known by kissers worldwide as the end of a perfect, or less than perfect, night. Other kisses are magic tools and a bit more mysterious, such as the Nuzzle. Whether they're famous or infamous, know your weapons and predicaments, and you'll be a kissing superstar.

The First Kiss

The most talked about, written about, and stressed about kiss on the planet, the First Kiss is the stuff that fond memories are made of. Or scary urban legends. It's usually thought of as the first kiss between would-be lovers but it can sometimes happen so spontaneously that it's as if you're not in control—the body is having its own fun while the brain spins its wheels in giddy confusion. A first kiss is a romantic kiss, and if it's shared between friends, it can change *everything*.

Great First Kisses

The Sweetheart Kiss
The Lusty Kiss
The Kama Sutra Kiss
The Mad Mack Attack Kiss

The Goodnight Kiss

At the end of the evening, when you and your date are about to part ways, it's time for the Goodnight Kiss. Sometimes this is the much-anticipated First Kiss, though it can also be a sweet thank-you for a nice evening, or a kiss known as the Taste of What's to Come. All humanoids know that a Goodnight Kiss can turn into so much more. That's why we like it. When this kiss is shared between friends who feel a spark of attraction beneath all that friendship mumbo jumbo, we see just how close two friends can get. If you want to stay neutral yet let him know you like him more than a pat on the back, a well-placed Goodnight Kiss lands on the cheek. If you want to send a direct message that you're attracted, plant a light one on the lips.

The Romantic Kiss

Everything is perfect—or not—for this intimate and compelling kiss. Romance is so much more than the setting—you can have a romantic kiss in a beautiful garden on a summer's day or at a bus stop in a crappy neighborhood. What matters is the intimacy, the connection, and the rose-colored glasses. When you both feel hot for each other and the whole world melts away, it's a Romantic Kiss, no matter where you are, who's watching, or what's going on around you. This kiss is all about the two of you, and it makes you the only two people in the world.

The Good-bye Kiss

This can be the fondest farewell, or the kiss-off, depending on how your date went. As a parting gesture it can be sweet and romantic, nervous and exciting, or a final sayonara that can be bittersweet or cold. Typically a kiss on the lips, it can also be a kiss on the cheek or forehead if you don't know him very well or want to keep your friendship within limits. Usually the "good-bye" is said while delivering the kiss—but some sneaky dates might turn the Good-bye Kiss on the cheek into a Romantic Kiss with a quick turn of the head. Be on guard!

The Sweetheart Kiss

Light like a butterfly, yet it sends electric shocks up and down his spine—this kiss is delivered sweetly and packs a punch. This is one of the more erotically potent kisses without getting too naughty. The Sweetheart Kiss is a style of kiss that can be delivered anywhere, anytime you want to focus his attraction to you. These are light, full-mouthed kisses, but with no tongue, planted on any exposed part of the body that looks inviting. Push your lips forward slightly, but keep them soft (and your mouth closed). Purse your lips, then press evenly with your upper and lower lip at the same time. These kisses should linger for only a moment or two, no more than the length of a full breath. After that, move to another technique or pull back. If you linger for a second, move your head slightly (instead of your lips) for a variation.

The Lusty Kiss

This is much like a Sweetheart Kiss, but with more pressure, and you linger as long as you want—make it last, and it'll be lusty. In addition, use your hands on his face, neck, and hair (unless he's a male model), and include subtle movements of your head—but no tongue yet. This is the kiss that lights his fire, a nice transition from Sweetheart-kissing to French-kissing (see below), and it says that you're ready to do more than peck each other on the lips or cheeks. Give this one when you're ready to really show 'em you want 'em bad, and you're willing to be bad to get what you want.

The Taste of What's to Come

Truly mischievous kissers of every gender know all about this kiss—and it's a secret weapon used by femmes fatales worldwide. This is the kiss that the female double agent gives James Bond so he doesn't blow her cover, the kiss that says you're as hot for him on the inside as you look on the outside. Often a full-mouthed French Kiss (see below), it has an urgency and lust matched by no other kiss; it shows him you've got more moves to make him melt than he can imagine. With this kiss you are the aggressor—you lead the kiss from beginning to end.

Pull him close, making eye contact. As you pull his lips to yours, slide your hands up to the back of his head (or cradle his neck if his hair is perfect), and press your body fully against his. Then leap into the kiss, pressing against him more as you pull him into you, firmly caressing his neck or head with your hands the whole time. French-kiss deeply, then pull away as you pull his head back. Smile wickedly, and continue eye contact.

The Kama Sutra Kiss

The Kama Sutra has long been revered as a source for romance and eroticism, being simultaneously sexual and subtle in its lingering appreciation of all the senses involved in a simple act of intimacy. The Kama Sutra Kiss, a nose-and-lips combination, is an excellent cuddling, sensual, and nuzzling kiss that can even be done in public without being too brazen. A sign of genuine affection, intimacy and tenderness, it can last from a few seconds to several minutes. The Kama Sutra can be done on any part of the body, but creases, folds, and bends, such as the nape of the neck, between the shoulder blades, behind the ears, and under the jaw, are ideal.

It's simple and feels sexy. Start by moving your lips close to the target area on his skin. Purse your lips for a kiss. Right when you make contact with skin, inhale and gently press your lips and nose into the skin, moving your head back and forth slightly to rub your face around on the spot. Give little Sweetheart Kisses as you nuzzle. This kiss is also wonderful for slowing down any bedroom action, deepening intimacy during lovemaking, or making a seduction into a pivotal take-down experience. It's like the "slow food movement" of kisses.

The Drunk Kiss

Sometimes confused with the Romantic Kiss, the Drunk Kiss happens more times then we want it to. It tastes like booze, makes you dizzy, and often leaves you with a sense of confusion and regret the next day (along with a pounding headache). Drunk Kisses are sloppy, drooling, and unattractive to passersby, yet for some reason you always think you look really glamorous and hot while you're going at it. In reality, to sober observers, you actually look like a Nature Channel documentary on gastropod mating—two pink slugs wrestling in slow motion under a waterfall. And if you can't remember it the next day, be certain that everyone else will.

Gladiator Kiss

This kiss is all him Tarzan, you Jane, and if you don't mind being moved around like a diminutive doll, when he's good at it, the Gladiator can be a pretty fun ride. Having a guy grab you and kiss you hard, as though he really means it, is hot, especially if he pulls you close and the kiss takes you by surprise—sometimes this is an instant turn-on. At worst, you'll feel as if you were being mauled by Bubba tryin' to "show the little lady how a man kisses." You are the conquest, and sure, it's all romantic in his eyes, but you might feel like a tenderized steak when he's done molesting your lips.

Mad Mack Attack Kiss

It's a stealth kiss. You sneak up on your kissing target and—smooch! Can be done on total strangers you find really hot (avoid Armed Services personnel and guys with bodybuilder girlfriends), or on your sweetie when you want to give him a naughty surprise. Afterward, you may choose to pretend that nothing happened, keep walking to the snack table, or stick around for his bewildered reaction.

French Kiss

The most famous kiss in the world is a full, open-mouthed kiss using tongue and lips together in perfect harmony— hopefully. You do not need to be French to deliver an excellent French Kiss. (And as of this writing, there is still no such thing as a Freedom Kiss.) The kiss begins with the meeting of slightly parted lips, then the lips open, and out come the tongues for a little *parlez-vous*. A side effect of

French-kissing is that both parties will have an increased amount of oral lubrication (read: drool), which is a turn-on for some and a gross-out for many others. Some kissers can French for seemingly hours and find it a wonderful pastime.

French-kissing can get pretty wet, so if slippery kisses don't float your boat, then alternate French Kisses with smooches on the neck, ears, and other kissable body parts. Sips of water also help—they give you a second to breathe and smile seductively before diving back in. French-kissing is also not limited to the mouth; some people find fun in Frenching their lover's ears and even the nose! One of the great things about the French Kiss is the creative freedom that comes with it: you can improvise, try out new techniques, or use a variety of techniques to craft your own French Kiss style. There are no rules for this kiss, other than that you enjoy it!

❀ Run your tongue around the teeth and gums
❀ Play with the tongue, taste it, push it around, caress it
❀ Nip at his teeth, lips, and tongue with your lips
❀ Kiss or probe deeply and gently with your tongue
❀ Apply suction on the tongue
❀ Dart your tongue in and out, slowly or rapidly
❀ Suck gently with your mouth
❀ Pull away slightly in midkiss, then go in for more

Angel Kisses

So light they almost tickle, these kisses are not done with your mouth, but rather with your eyelashes. Angel Kisses consist of fluttering your eyelash against a sensitive (and sexy) body part to deliver a feathery tickle. Popular Angel Kiss spots include his cheek, lips, eyelids, ears, neck, nipples, and genitals.

Eskimo Kisses

A playful favorite for many lovers, these kisses are done with the nose instead of the mouth. Typically, you and your partner rub noses together in an Eskimo Kiss. But see the Kama Sutra Kiss (above) for techniques on other parts of the body.

Snuggle Bunny Kisses

So romantic, so cute—this is the ultimate in intimate, loving kisses. You don't need to be in love to share Snuggle Bunnies; you share these nuzzling, closed-mouthed, soft-lipped pecks and smooches of all kinds, on exposed areas of skin, when you're lying down, wrapped around each other, at a tender, quiet moment. These signify extreme affection for one another. They are perfect before and after sex, in front of a fire or TV, or even on a picnic blanket in a public place.

Scary Kisses

Kissing isn't always butterflies and bunnies—there are kisses (and kissers) out there that make us want to flee. Or at least will have you checking your watch midway through what started as a sexy smooch but turned into the longest twenty seconds of your life.

But what if you really like the guy? Teach him what you like in kissing. Play a kissing version of follow-the-leader: tell him to do exactly what you do. Reward good behavior with yummy noises, moaning, squeezes with your hands. Discourage deviation from your lesson by pulling back to stop the kiss.

Is he a scary smoocher?
Learn to identify these hazardous kisses:

The Fish Tank Kiss: Every girl's nightmare. He's totally cute, funny, the conversation is good—but then you kiss and it feels like he's trying to clean the inside of your mouth as if it was a fish tank. As the minutes pass more slowly than you ever thought possible, you wonder if he's actually looking for treasure. His tongue is too hard, and it darts about quickly and all pokey. You are usually too stunned to decide whether you should wait it out or hold up a "send help" sign. Toss this one back into the sea.

The Chewing Gum Kiss: You've seen these before—a couple joined at the mouth, lips locked in a deep French-kissing session that looks like they're about to gnaw each other's head off. Don't worry, everyone will be fine, but this combination of French Kiss and Fish Tank Kiss with extreme jaw movement looks pretty scary if you watch too many horror movies.

The Limp Noodle: So sad, the Noodle. When you lock lips and start to French, and his lips just hang there and his tongue lies there like a slug, you have a Limp Noodle on your hands. No matter how much you push, massage, and prod his tongue to bring it back to life, it plays possum, dead in the middle of the road. There is nothing you can do—you're basically giving mouth-to-mouth to this guy.

Mercy Kisses

Sometimes you kiss for fun, and sometimes you just have to give a kiss out of pity—hence the Mercy Kiss. You give these kisses when you feel bad about something, want your date to look good (even though you aren't into him), or just feel sorry for the poor sap. Only in the movies do these kisses turn into a blazing romance. If you end up on the receiving end of a Mercy Kiss, just enjoy it and then excuse yourself to go wash your cat.

The Zombie Kiss

Another nightmare kiss many of us have experienced, which seems to come from beyond the grave. It's as if all the life drains out of him as he comes in for a kiss: the eyes flutter, clamp shut, or roll back into his head. His face goes slack and lifeless. And the most horrifying part of all: his mouth opens up into a gaping maw, threatening to swallow you whole. Sometimes the Zombie Kisser comes at you like a lost extra from *Night of the Living Dead*, mouth agape, with a shiny pink sluglike tongue pointing out at you. Scream! Run! Barricade the doors and windows!

The Zoolander Kiss

Ever wonder what it would be like to kiss an international male model? The Zoolander makes you feel like you're a pretty prop designed to make him look good as he poses, shifts, and gives his "sexy" face to the world while kissing you. Would he notice if you were gone? Probably not. The Zoolander Kiss is meant purely to compliment the physical beauty of the man kissing you—it's not for anyone's actual physical pleasure. It's used when trying to impress others or to make someone jealous.

Chapter 5:

DELIVER A KNOCKOUT KISS

The kiss that conquers all is your key to paradise—so it's important to have a full arsenal of techniques at your disposal. Anyone would be lucky to plant one on your lips—especially when you've got the skills to make him melt.

It's all about style, delivery, and hot spots. With a range of methods to choose among you can develop your own kissing style. Depending on how you feel, or how hot you want him to feel, you can start with nibbles, progress to licks, and on to passionate lip presses. Or make it hotter by adding light lip suction and tongue-to-tongue caresses. Meanwhile, between techniques, you can whisper sweet nothings into his mouth, exciting him even more.

You'll want to know a full range of techniques so you can adjust your style to match that of your partner—an extremely valuable skill. For instance, if your kissing partner starts out lightly grazing your lips, will you know how to return the kiss—or how to gently take it to the next level? Then, when your kissing session really heats up, use advanced, expert tricks to show him you're a make-out master. And don't forget that great kissing isn't just about using your mouth—it's about making the most of your hands and body movements and smooching those sexy hot spots all over his body.

Techniques

Kissing techniques come in three main categories: light, intermediate, and intense. Lighter techniques are perfect for first kisses, short kisses, starting out a kissing session, cooling off a particularly hot encounter, and ending a kiss. Intermediate techniques are yummy filling—use these for the duration, mixed liberally with light or intense techniques, depending on how you want the make-out session to go. Intense techniques are exactly that—serious turn-ons, secret weapons, the techniques you pull out when there's no turning back.

In your kissing sessions, try a sequence of light kisses, followed by intermediate, then intense, then a brief pause, and repeat. People with glasses might want to take them off for an extended kissing session, and people with orthodontic braces will want to take care not to press too hard. Experiment with tempo and pacing. Practice the following techniques on the palm of your hand (the sensitive hollow, in the middle), then on a very lucky test subject.

Appetizers

Nibble. Nibbles are little bites using only your lips, or your upper lip with your tongue. When you nibble on a part of the body, lightly nip or squeeze the skin between your lips. You can nibble lightly, or with as much force as your lips can muster—either way, the sensations will be pleasant. You can nibble anyplace on the body that sticks out: lips, nose, earlobes, nipples, or on wider expanses of skin such as cheeks, neck, chest, and stomach.

Graze. When you graze an area of his body, you simply brush your lips over it. This can be done with small, short movements, or long, wide strokes. Imagine your lips as a paintbrush. Try slow strokes or quick circles. A pair of lips can graze any area of his body, and this is a very sexy way to get acquainted with the scent of your sweetie's skin.

Trace. Similar in technique to grazing, tracing can be done in all the same ways, but instead using the tip of your tongue. Trace around his lips as if applying lip balm, or trace strokes, shapes, and patterns on other parts of his body—especially any hot spots.

Breathe together. With both mouths open, nothing is sexier than inhaling someone's breath—literally taking his breath away. Take turns.

Sweet kisses. These are light, full-mouthed kisses, but with no tongue. Push your lips forward slightly, but keep them soft (and your mouth closed). Try your best to press evenly with your upper and lower lip at the same time. These kisses should linger for only a moment or two, no more than the length of a full breath. Purse your lips, then press, then move to another technique or pull back. If you linger for a second, move your head slightly (instead of your lips) for a variation.

Dish of the Day

Speak. Whispering or speaking gently into your partner's open mouth between kisses is incredibly arousing. Tell him how much you enjoy what you're doing, how good his lips/tongue/kisses feel, how sexy he looks kissing you, or how excited you are. You can even tell him where you want him to touch or kiss you, if you're feeling daring. Moaning into his mouth is also extremely hot.

Lip presses. These are similar to "Sweet Kisses" above, but without any movement, and more pressure. It sounds simple, yet it is very effective in focusing his attention on your desire—this technique communicates sensual direct-ness. Purse your lips, press firmly against his lips, pull back. Repeat more slowly, controlling the kiss.

Bottom lip/top lip. This technique focuses your attentions on his top or bottom lip. You can play with one at a time, or single out one for extra-special attention. The popular lip for this technique is the bottom one, but the top lip is equally sexy and intimate to engage. Lick the lip you choose, nibble it, graze it, suck, and even give it a tiny bite.

Corners of the mouth. Don't neglect the corners of his mouth when you're kissing—it's easy to forget when you have a pair of sexy lips to nibble on! The corner is where the lips meet, at the edges. This is a highly sensitive area, and it deserves the sweetest kisses, lip presses, licks, and nibbles—but it is so sensitive that you shouldn't overdo it.

Open mouth, no tongue. A terrific transition technique that can be used over and over at every stage. Open your mouth a little (never open wide) and kiss wetly, with a lot of lip motion. It's tempting to let your tongue poke out just a bit, but this kiss is much sexier (and there's less saliva) when you keep it in your mouth. Push, suck, pull, rub, and massage with your open lips, but never cover his whole mouth with yours or it'll have a suffocating effect that many people detest.

Roof of the mouth. This is a highly controversial kissing area because it is so sensitive. Some guys like having the roof of the mouth lightly licked—and if your kissee does, then do it a little, and back off. Others might dislike the sensation because it feels like a tickle, and they'll want to scratch it. Of course, if you're playing mischievous sex games and teasing each other, tickling the roof of his mouth is a sexy and highly intimate way to "get his goat."

Dessert
Suck. I touched on light to moderate suction in earlier techniques, but when you're playing for higher stakes, creating

a vacuum with your lips and mouth sends a direct message of sex to your lover. Keep your lips soft and create a seal with your mouth, removing the air a little, or a lot. Suck lips, teeth, tongue, neck—it doesn't have to be a perfect seal, and you can slip around playfully and even make a few sexy noises while you're at it.

Lick. Moisten your tongue before you lick, but be sure that it isn't too wet—we all know how awful a slurpy lick can be. Point your tongue yet keep it soft (practice!), and brush it across his lips, lick the corners of his mouth, lick under his chin (if he's not too stubbly). Lick the neck, ears, and nape (base) of the neck. Use wide, flat strokes on wide areas. Make circles, spell words, or press with your tongue as you lick. You can even lick his teeth and tongue.

Probe. This technique consists of inserting your tongue into his mouth and slowly, sensuously exploring the teeth and tongue, or the whole of his mouth. Don't rush this one, or use a hardened tongue, or the technique will backfire. Take your time and savor every moment, every flavor, every sensation.

Tongue only. This is a no-lip, tongue-only kissing technique. It will make you giggle and smile, or it will make you both very aroused. Make eye contact before you move in for the kiss, opening your lips in a half-smile and extending your tongue in an upward curve. When you reach his tongue, keep your tongue out of your mouth and play your two tongues together, taking a long time to feel the textures and flavor of his tongue, and have fun dancing your tongues around together.

French-kissing. Like the tongue-only technique, but advanced. This is an open-mouthed, full-contact kiss with both tongues completely engaged. Purse and press your lips together to begin the kiss, then, at the moment of contact, part your lips and sneak a gentle lick of his lips with your tongue. If his lips part (I bet they will), gently slip your tongue past his lips to taste his tongue. You may pull your tongue back and disengage to repeat the whole kiss over again, or you can linger and continue French-kissing. Touch and caress each other's tongues, taking a long time to feel and sense textures and tastes. Lick the center of his tongue, and the sides. Lick his front teeth, upper and lower. Take your time, and enjoy varying the pressure of your tongue and lips. Don't forget to keep your lips in gentle motion—with this technique, "frozen" or hard lips feel weird.

Rock Your Body

You're not just a pair of lips and a tongue when you're engaged in a kiss—you have much more at your fingertips (literally) to stimulate your sweetie with and keep him riveted to your lips. Use your hands to touch his shoulders and neck, hold his cheeks (on his face, ahem), or cradle the back of his head. You can caress or grab, knead or massage. Stroke his hair, or if your passions are high, run your hands through his hair, or all over his sexy bald head, should that be the case. Touching his face will be a big, highly charged (and amazingly intimate) turn-on, so caress the forehead, eyes, cheekbones, jawline, even the lips, all while you are kissing. Keep your hands in motion throughout your kissing session.

Eye contact is also extremely important, though when your faces are very close you will want to close your eyes. The more eye contact you make between kisses, the more intense your kisses will become. When your heads come together for a kiss, close your eyes just at the point you feel your eyes straining, to avoid giving him a lingering view of you with your eyes crossed!

A little movement behind the kiss feels heavenly. Move

your head just a little as you kiss—but not so much that he has a hard time following your lips. Subtle movements will change the angle of your lips slightly, resulting in a very passionate kiss. The more intense your kissing becomes, the more you can nuzzle and push with your head and lips—his reactions will tell you to keep going, or you can follow his lead. If he wants you to keep going, he'll return your push with enthusiasm, a return push, or even a little moan.

Don't forget to smile between, and during, kisses. Smiling is extremely seductive, and it lets him know you're really enjoying yourself. And, occasionally, stop kissing and enjoy the pause that refreshes: hold his head in your hands, gaze into his eyes for a count of four, then resume kissing.

Hot Spots
Also known as erogenous zones, hot spots on the body make terrifically sensuous places to use your kissing techniques. While genitals are definitely an erogenous zone, I have left them out of the discussion for the purposes of this book.

Cheek. Kissing, grazing, and nuzzling the cheek feels wonderful and is almost guaranteed to make anyone smile. A light peck on the cheek can be a friendly greeting, a good-bye, or an excellent first-date kiss.

Ears. Kisses, licks, and gentle sucking can drive some guys absolutely wild. This is a serious hot spot, and even the lightest breath here will send shivers up his spine, raise ample goose bumps, and generally get instant attention. Some men become extremely aroused when you lick their ears or suck on an earlobe. Be highly aware that everything you do near an ear is very, very loud.

Eyes. There's something uniquely tender about kissing someone's closed eyelid. Not many people do it, but it's very pleasant and quite unforgettable. Give him sweet kisses on his (closed) eyelids, eyebrows, the outside corners of the eyes, or just beneath the eyes.

Fingers and hands. Grab a hand and kiss and lick the upturned palm, or kiss, lick, and suck the fingertips. This technique is a man-melter, especially if you simulate fellatio on a finger (or fingers), while making eye contact.

Feet and toes. Admittedly not a technique for everyone, yet one that some people really love giving and receiving. Some might get so turned on by having their (clean) feet kissed (top and underside), or having their toes sucked, or the sole of their foot licked, that they can barely control themselves. Others may be too ticklish or too self-conscious about their feet to enjoy it. Ask first. If he likes it, you can also rub his foot on your face and neck (or breasts!), and massage a foot as you kiss.

Forehead. A very tender, romantic place to kiss. A kiss here says, *I care about you.*

Neck. Like the ears, the neck is super sensitive and a sexually supercharged place to kiss. Lick, kiss, nibble, graze, even suck and bite on it—though be aware that your kissee may not want you to leave any marks. Make his neck a canvas for all the different brushstrokes your tongue can paint, and remember that the harder you press with lips and tongue, the more aroused he'll get.

Shoulders. An often-neglected area for kissing that communicates romance and tenderness. Not as sensitive as the neck, the shoulders do respond erotically to kisses, and they can give any human deep shivers.

Chapter 6:

THE RULES OF THE GAME

It's impossible to pick a great kisser out of a crowd. You just never know who's got the sweetest smooches until you kiss, and you certainly can't tell by looking. The only true way to know is to take the leap and kiss the toads—and know what to do when everything goes wrong. We all know what to do when things go right: enjoy it, relax, go back for more, and more! Unfortunately, things don't always go so great and it's good to have a backup plan in case your make-out session turns into a make-out catastrophe.

If the hottie you finally get to kiss turns out to be a dud kisser, you need to decide whether it's worth continuing or you should execute your exit strategy. This has happened to every girl and boy alive, and how you deal with it can change your partner's kissing habits for the better, or teach you how to pick a better kisser next time. Sometimes, it's our own approach that spoils the mood or turns a romantic kiss into a tragicomedy. Know your etiquette for every kissing scenario, and you can't go wrong.

Kissing Do's and Don'ts

Kissing is one of life's greatest pleasures that can be shared by two. But not everyone is a perfect kissing match, and certainly not all kissers are created equal. Sadly, we encounter over a lifetime of kissing quite a few kissers who make elementary—or truly awful—kissing *faux pas*, and it makes us wish that everyone with a pair of lips got their own user's manual.

Wouldn't it be great if there was a mandatory kissing politeness class in every high school? Here students would learn that kissing isn't a face-chewing contest. You do not get points for trying to box the tonsils with your tongue. Licking your lips too suggestively before a kiss looks really scary and gross. And above all, kissing is something you do together, rather than to or at another person.

It might be a very long time until kissing etiquette becomes required for graduation into the real world. Until then, there are a few things to know that will keep you and those you kiss happy to be smooched. Show the following list to anyone you know who might benefit from the advice it offers. Even a friend who's dating someone she just discovered is a bad kisser—it might give her some ideas.

❀Beautiful, brushed teeth, fresh breath, and supple, moisturized lips make you a delight to kiss. Anything less is a drag.

❀It's okay to pull away and take a break from kissing without saying anything. It's okay for someone to want to stop completely and offer no explanation. You can talk about it later.

❀It's not okay to expect a kiss in return for anything. Kisses are gifts, not currency.

❀Cradling your partner's head and face feels wonderful. As long as you're not trying to prevent escape or contributing to claustrophobia.

❀Kissing isn't the checkered flag and starter gun to feel up your date. Lip contact is not an invitation to ass grabbing or unhooking a bra. The good bits aren't going anywhere, and it is in your best interest to take your time.

❀A kiss does not signify a willingness to have sex, ever— no matter what kind of kiss.

❀Never approach a kiss with an open mouth, or with an extended tongue.

❀Never open your mouth wider than your kissing partner's lips.

❀Poking with your tongue is annoying. You are not trying to make a phone call.

❀Not everyone will like the things you like, and that's okay. You may love to have your sensitive ears licked and breathed on, but he might hate it with a passion. Be open to all kissing styles.

❀Whenever you're in doubt about how things feel for your kissing partner, or even if it's the right time to kiss, ask. Your partner will be happy you care enough to ask.

About Hickeys and Love Bites

In previous sections about biting and sucking, I've cautioned about leaving marks on his skin, also known as hickeys or love bites. These marks happen when teeth bruise the skin or suction leaves a rashlike discoloration on the skin. The suction created by your mouth draws blood to the surface of the skin, breaking the little capillaries, and scraping your teeth over the skin makes them break even more, blossoming into blood bruises that can range in color from pink to purple.

Overall, it's very bad for your skin and the nerve endings, and some say it can cause nerve damage. But for people who love these marks, and the way it feels to get a hickey, it's not a huge concern. Often these marks are made unknowingly—it can be totally unintentional, a result of passion. People with sensitive skin or those who bruise easily will get hickeys often from little stimulation of their skin.

Not everyone wants marks from kissing. The reasons can be many, including looking improper at work—bosses, office mates, and customers may find hickeys offensive or unprofessional. If he asks you not to leave visible marks on his neck, do not take it personally or try to second-guess his reasons. It may seriously compromise his work environment or professional reputation, or he just may not want marks on his neck for the entire world to see. Family members tend to frown on hickeys, as do officials, so if he's going to be appearing in court, seeing valuable or new clients, working in sales, or visiting relatives, be careful.

In general, it's a no-no to leave marks in visible places but forgivable in hidden spots. This varies from person to person. He simply might not like the way they look. Be sure to ask him how he feels about love bites before your kisses start to stray away from his mouth, and he'll be able to relax knowing he's with a considerate kisser.

Kiss Catastrophes and Remedies

There are great moments in kissing—and then, most unfortunately, there are moments we simply wish had happened to someone else. Kisses should be shared, savored, mutually enjoyed. But sometimes that garlic you had for dinner turns into a horrifying burp, or you collide painfully when you wanted to connect soulfully, or the guy you thought might be a kissing artist is a kissing ingrate, a slobbery mess. What to do? Consult the following kissing cures and you'll be smooching a suitable partner like your sexy-bad self again in no time.

What went wrong: You went in for a kiss and he said no.

Treatment: It's almost impossible to believe he could resist your wiles—and yet somehow, he did. Do not fret or take it personally. Did he tell you why? If not, ask. Believe what he tells you and take it at face value as the truth, and decide later if you think he (or his answer) is for real—while you decide if he's still worth it.

What went wrong: You have an awful rash from his stubble.

Treatment: See the next chapter for beard burn solutions.

What went wrong: Your mouth slobbered too much at the wrong moment.

Treatment: It happens to the best kissers among us. We taste something good and our mouths overflow in the most ungrateful way. Apologize, smile, and laugh it off. Jokingly offer him a napkin.

What went wrong: Burps or hiccups (yours) during a kiss. Worse, other gases are expelled.

Treatment: This is one of the most embarrassing of bodily mishaps. All you can think is Body! How can you betray me so?! Since these things are involuntary and we have little or no control over them, all you can do is say "oops," smile, and laugh at the foul cards you have been dealt (hopefully not too foul, or you'll want to suggest kissing in a different room, or in a wind tunnel).

What went wrong: He turned out to be an awful kisser.

Treatment: Consider whether he is good enough overall to retrain and keep. If not, it's time to say goodnight. Politely end the kiss with a smile and a few small parting pecks (try to avoid hurting his feelings with your sighs of disappointment), and thank him for a nice time.

What went wrong: You want him to go away!

Treatment: Moan really, really loud while kissing. Keep your eyes open and let your eyeballs roll up into your head with ecstasy. Between kisses, rock to and fro while humming. Continue your *Exorcist* impersonation as needed. Alternatively, say an abrupt "Thanks!" and be on your merry way.

What went wrong: You had gum in your mouth, you hid it, and he found it.

Treatment: Fess up on the spot. Ask if he is horrified. Tell him *you* are. Instantly get over it. Continue kissing.

What went wrong: You bit a little too hard.

Treatment: Did you give an unwanted surprise, or did you actually draw blood? Say you're sorry that you're so hungry and suggest that you adjourn for a snack (unless you have to apply a tourniquet to his tongue or face).

What went wrong: You went in for a kiss too fast and bonked heads/noses/teeth.

Treatment: Giggle. Laugh. Pretend it hurt you a little more than it really did, and apologize. Ask if you can try again, and act silly about being extra careful.

What went wrong: He keeps doing something you don't enjoy or that annoys you.

Treatment: If you want to keep kissing him, gently let him know you don't fancy the painfully hard lip sucking. Or if it's something really annoying, stop the kissing altogether and be upfront about what's bugging you. Chances are good you're not the first to be bugged by this particular behavior, but you might be the first to let him know about it. This is helpful to him in the long run; you're doing him a favor. You can also politely suggest an alternate behavior: "You know, I really like to start kisses with both mouths closed and work up to tongues after a long time. Can we try it my way for a little while?"

Chapter 7

TAKE YOUR KISSING
TO THE NEXT LEVEL

Being a great kisser isn't just knowing the techniques of a good kiss, though that certainly helps. No, what transforms a good kiss into a badass, knee-buckling experience is having a few wicked tricks ready for action, anytime. Want to make him do a double-take the next time you kiss? Or make that first kiss the most arousing he's ever tasted by giving it a little twist he's never experienced?

Don't just make yourself the master of the kiss with advanced tricks and treats. Be a kiss guru to lovers and friends by learning tricks that are turn-ons and tricks that make kissing more pleasant for everyone. Tell your friends how to give kisses that taste like their lover's favorite candy, or be the bringer of sage advice on how to cope with stubble and the rash from mega mack sessions that result in beard burn.

Best of all, these tricks and treats make your kissing world a lot spicier. Make your kisses legendary, the stuff of campfire tales, with advanced kissing techniques passed down through the ages from secret kissing societies and kissing masters, revealed here for the very first time.

Tricks and Treats

Cold. Chill the temperature of your mouth with ice or a cold drink before a kiss. Ice cream cools and flavors your mouth. You can even pass an ice cube mouth to mouth. This is a fun surprise trick.

Heat. Make your mouth very warm before a kiss for an exciting surprise. Swish a hot beverage around for a second or two, swallow, then give him a kiss.

Tickle. Point your tongue into a hard tip and use it to tickle any area you like by flickering it in short, rapid movements.

Bite. Easy, now—take small, light bites with your teeth on lips, tongue, or areas of skin. Start very light, and be aware that some guys may not want you to bite them at all, or to leave marks (for a variety of reasons). If he appears to like it (moaning, pushing into your mouth), bite just a little bit harder. Give him almost what he wants—then a little bit more.

Underwater. While swimming, pull him under the surface for a smooch. The cold water will intensify the warmth of your mouths, and the water around the seal your mouths make feels amazing. A fun variation is kissing in the shower or under a waterfall.

Upside down. This is a lot of fun, and a very playful way to kiss. No one has to hang from a fire escape like Spider-Man (though it looks like fun), and it doesn't take a lot of coordination. One of you hangs your head off the edge of a bed, over the arm of a couch, or off the side of a swimming pool, and see what it's like to match mouths upside down.

Tongue suction. This is a very naughty trick—you essentially treat your partner's tongue as if it were a sensual lollipop, and give a little gentle in-and-out suction. Make a small O shape with your mouth around his tongue, apply a little suction, and slide your lips back and forth, up and down his tongue. Vary your suction and rhythm, and pause intermittently to let the sensations sink in.

Sharing a drink. Have you ever really *shared* a drink? Hold a small amount of delicious drink, such as Champagne or ambrosial fruit juice, in your mouth, and when you kiss, let a sip drain into his mouth. The sexier the beverage, the better. Daring kissers can employ this technique from above, letting the liquid literally drip into his waiting mouth. To start, sip the liquid, kiss him, let a little bit slip into his mouth, then pull away as more liquid comes out. If it gets messy, lick it off his lips, chin, and neck.

Sharing candy. Decadent and delicious, nothing beats a slow-melting piece of butterscotch or peppermint shared by two. Pop it in your mouth, enjoy, and then pass it with a kiss. After a while, ask for it back. Repeat until the candy is gone. You can do this over the course of a party, movie, or make-out session. Can also be done with chewing gum.

Sizzling candy. Some candies "pop" or fizz when they make contact with the wet surface of your tongue. Shared by two, these candies can give a French Kiss quite a kick.

Wind tunnel. Suck the air from your partner's mouth, either slowly or rapidly, depending on the mood. Breathe hot air back in. This can progress to breathing into each other's mouth, a highly charged, sexy game.

Swap techniques. Tell him you want to be kissed using a technique he really enjoys receiving, then switch and kiss him in one of the ways you really like to be kissed. This is a fantastic way to learn what he likes and to show him what techniques you like best.

A Smooch with a View: Best Movie Kisses to Watch Together for Inspiration

A Room with a View, Helena Bonham Carter and
   Julian Sands
She's ambushed in a field of beautiful flowers.

Blade Runner, Harrison Ford and Sean Young
Sexy, beat-up tough guy kissing scene that sizzles.

Bull Durham, Susan Sarandon and Kevin Costner
An outrageous build-up to an outrageous kiss.

Casablanca, Humphrey Bogart and Ingrid
   Bergman
A searing good-bye kiss.

Gone with the Wind, Clark Gable and Vivien Leigh
The ultimate conflict-turned-passionate kiss.

The Matrix Reloaded, Keanu Reeves and Monica Bellucci
She wants to know what Neo's true love (Trinity) experiences when they kiss.

Notorious, Cary Grant and Ingrid Bergman
Long, unusual, playful, arousing.

Sixteen Candles, Molly Ringwald and Michael Schoeffling
Unforgettable, like many first kisses.

Some Kind of Wonderful, Mary Stuart Masterson and Eric Stoltz
Kissing lessons that turn into much more.

Spider-Man, Kirsten Dunst and Tobey Maguire
Deep superhero kisses after a heroic battle can't be beat.

Some Other Hot Make-out Flicks

Belle de Jour
Henry and June
Dangerous Liaisons
Secretary (kinky)
Eyes Wide Shut
The Scent of Green Papaya
Y tu mamá también

Flavored Kisses

Do you taste good? Flavor your mouth with candy, tasty herbs (mint, basil, fennel), ice cream, or a drink of something delicious. He'll never forget that kiss if it tastes like butterscotch, peppermint, chocolate, or even something more exotic like basil, tamarind, or vanilla. Some will even get a charge out of the flavor of coffee or wine. But your kissee won't be back for more if your mouth is stale or tastes like an ashtray.

When you know you'll be with someone you want to kiss, keep flavorful items nearby to make your mouth yummier. In a pinch, at a restaurant or bar, you can chew on a variety of garnishes readily available—some might even be in your cocktail glass or sitting demurely on the edge of your dinner plate.

Flavor Psychology

To be: cool
Nibble: mint

To be: sassy
Nibble: lemon

To be: playful
Nibble: lime

To be: brazen
Nibble: basil leaves

To be: mischievous
Nibble: parsley

To be: feisty
Nibble: ginger

To be: naughty
Nibble: a cherry

To be: dirty
Nibble: an olive

Some items might sound good for flavoring your mouth but are really a bad idea. These include mouthwash (especially Listerine), cough drops, garlic, nuts and seeds (too grainy, yuck), Cheetos, and artificially flavored drinks or snacks, which often leave a sour aftertaste. Never try to cover up strong flavors (such as the garlic you ate at dinner) with gum or mints—it never works, and tastes really gross.

Kissing Flavor Favorites

❀ mints—Altoids are intense!
❀ butterscotch candy
❀ red wine
❀ Champagne
❀ peaches
❀ cassis
❀ vanilla
❀ chocolate
❀ watermelon
❀ cinnamon
❀ licorice
❀ bubble gum
❀ honey
❀ sex

It's important to keep in mind that there might be flavor factors going on in your body that can adversely affect your flavor from within. Multivitamins can make your mouth taste like a health food store. Antihistamines (and drugs in general, be they prescription or otherwise) can make you taste like chemicals. And strong foods such as curries, garlic, asparagus, broccoli, beets, and red meats will affect your flavor as well. Cigarettes will make you taste like tobacco at best, and like an ashtray at worst.

You can, of course, sweeten yourself from within. If you take vitamins or antihistamines, try to drink lots of water and citrus juices to neutralize the funk these pills leave behind. Make your essence sweeter by adding citrus and other fruits, honey, and cucumber to your diet. Pineapple, lemon, lime, mango, papaya, banana, fresh ginger, and vanilla all make you taste great, and a few days of drinking creative smoothies with these ingredients will make your mouth into a decadent, kissable dessert.

Flavored Lipsticks and Gloss

Remember junior high school, when the big thing was gooey-sweet strawberry lip gloss? Well, times have changed, and today's flavored and scented lipsticks and glosses come in a variety of consistencies, colors, and flavors. To see a selection of the yummy treats you can spike your smooches with, take a trip to your nearest department store cosmetics counter or to Sephora. There are over a dozen makeup brands with gloss flavors in everything from latte to raspberry frosting, even chocolate martini. These lines of lip glosses add light sparkle and shine while flavoring and scenting your lips with candy flavors such as caramel, cherry, mocha, and more. And to make your kisses more alluring and interesting, the gloss in most of these products plumps up your lips a bit and tingles—a sensation that can be felt by both kissers.

MAC makes vanilla gloss, and Stila has passion fruit, watermelon, lime, and more. On the opposite end of the spectrum is the daily wear lipstick by Chanel, which is not flavored but smells literally like roses, a far cry from stinky, waxy-smelling drugstore shades.

Flavored glosses and lipsticks make your lips smell inviting and taste sweet, but they're not for everyone. A fresh application combined with a heavy make-out session will have you both sticky from ear to ear, a natural, sometimes fun consequence, but one to consider. Some guys don't like lipsticks or glosses on their kissing partners, preferring to kiss *au naturel* instead.

When in doubt, ask. And don't forgo something you

really like for the sake of only one guy. On the other hand, many men will enjoy that you went the extra step to make kissing a little sexier, a little naughtier, and they won't mind a little stickiness for the sake of good, not-too-clean fun. If he's worried about messing it up, tell him you've got plenty more where that came from.

You're not limited to lip gloss if you want add an extra something to your kisses, and you don't have to color your lips if you only want to play around with scent or sensation. Lip moisturizers often contain menthols that cool and tingle your lips, resulting in a decadent icy-hot feeling. And when you kiss, it's a sensation shared by two! Look for brands such as Carmex and Blistex Medicated. Last, but not least, if you're looking to shine up your lips by adding glitter, know that it will turn your kisses into an abrasive, exfoliating, grit-in-the-teeth experience.

Set the Mood with Music to Make Out By

"A Love Supreme," by John Coltrane
"Avalon," by Roxy Music
"Dummy," by Portishead
"Endtroducing," by DJ Shadow
"Exile," by Gary Newman
"Fear of Fours," by Lamb
"Heaven or Las Vegas" and "Victorialand,"
by Cocteau Twins
"Into the Night," by Julee Cruise
"Kind of Blue" and "Sketches of Spain," by Miles Davis
"Ki Oku," by DJ Krush
"Le roi est mort," by Enigma
"Let's Get Lost," by Chet Baker
"Mezzanine," by Massive Attack
"Passion Soundtrack," by Peter Gabriel
"Play," by Moby
"So Tonight that I Might See," by Mazzy Star
"Telegraph," by Bjork
any album by Al Green
any album by Barry White
any album by Billie Holliday

Stubble Burn—and How to Avoid It

When he nuzzles your neck like a big happy kitty and he has just a hint of stubble, it can feel delicious in that scratchy-rough-yummy kind of way. But if you smooch for any period of time and he has short, prickly stubble, it can become quite uncomfortable and leave you with an angry burn—on your face and lips! Exfoliation, the hard way. The more vigorous, intense, and extended the session, the higher your risk for rash. Some men grow facial hair faster than others, and a number of guys have stubble that seems razor sharp the minute it pokes out of his skin. When he's so kissable you have to throw caution to the wind, there are a few things both of you can do to ease the sting of stubble burn.

First, know that a mack session with a stubbly guy is going to be like using a dry exfoliant on your face and lips. Try to go into the kissing session without washing or moisturizing your face, as your tender or moist face will just make you more susceptible to irritation. Afterward, wash your face and lips gently with a soothing cleanser and pat dry. Apply a moisturizer that is noncomedogenic, fragrance-free, and doesn't contain any mineral oils; otherwise, your face will break out or become irritated. If you're bright red and feeling the burn more than usual, use a moisturizer with aloe vera. Don't exfoliate the areas for at least two days.

There are many things he can do to help. He should be shaving with a really good, brand-new razor: opinions are heavily in favor of the Gillette Mach 3. Of course, if he skips a day or two of shaving, the stubble will be much softer and more comfortable to kiss than fresh stubble. Very short stubble, say, about 5–10 hours old, can be the most painful type, as the hairs are at their shortest and most inflexible. Ideally, he should skip a day of shaving, and then take great care to soften the stubble with hot water, hot towels, or even an application of hair conditioner.

Both parties should use a good lip salve afterward to condition the lips and help them heal. Blistex Clear Advance is the most highly recommended in this category.

Chapter 8

THE MAKE-OUT ARTIST

Being a make-out artist is all about style and confidence. Armed with the tips presented in this guide, you now have dozens of foolproof techniques for kissing your man *du jour* from start to finish—even better, from head to toe. As a freshly styled kissing artist, you don't need to set your sights on world domination or creating an army of male slaves. Perhaps you're just tired of being the "good girl" kisser, and you'd like to be the man-magnet for a change. Or maybe you're on the prowl for a down-and-dirty fling.

You don't even have to be a saucy dresser to be a first-rate kisser; you can employ your powers to attract, seduce, and kiss unforgettably anytime, anyplace, in any guise. This chapter will help you put your newfound tools together to become a femme fatale kisser: chemistry, technique, subtle manipulation through body language, and of course, mind control. This is going to make you a legendary make-out artist.

Create a Connection

In chapter 1 of this book I talked about chemistry and making a connection with your physical cues. To get the make-out session started, it's all about the messages you send—your body language gives him the right idea. Focus that language through your eyes. Even though you've got the techniques rehearsed and have styled those prettied-up lips to perfection, eye contact is truly the focus of all your efforts. Every move you make hinges on what you do with your eyes. If you keep your eyes closed in movie-kiss imitation bliss, no guy will think you are interested—or *interesting*—for real.

Anyone can make out by pretending to surrender to the moment with dreamy closed eyes, or staring at his lips (preferably not at the floor, or the clock)—but an artful lover makes eye contact whenever possible. Not all the time; as with driving, you'll want to keep your eyes moving. Direct them to the places you want him to think you find interesting, like his lips and neck, and where he puts his hands—

but always come back to the center of who he is: his eyes. Most important of all, this will make him feel special and draw him in even closer.

Reel him in like a fish, and keep smiling. The easiest way to disarm, relax, and intrigue a man is with a smile. Even a light smile while kissing will make you appear that much more inviting. As you kiss, let a smile dance constantly on your lips. This really turns guys on: knowing he's the one making you smile is an instant hook. It boosts his ego like crazy. A smile also sends him the message that you have a great sense of humor, you're approachable and open, and being around you is safe and a good time.

Keep Your Confidence High

He might be making the moves, but you're really the one in the driver's seat at all times—and you know it. While making out, stay aware of how you look from the outside. Borrow bits and pieces of your kissing moves from kissing scenes in films you think are hot. (See chapter 7, "A Smooch with a View: Best Movie Kisses to Watch Together for Inspiration.") If you ever get a chance to peep at another couple making out, watch skilled kissers and sexy vixens closely to see how they smile, make eye contact, hold their heads, and laugh. These skills are a snap to make your own. Take mental notes, and try them out.

Make your make-out strategies "idiot proof" by going over the techniques in this book step by step, repeatedly, and don't leave anything to the last minute. Prepare yourself carefully to make sure you feel comfortable beforehand: you feel sexy in your outfit, you have a few topics to chat about, and you have a backup plan if the make-out session fizzles.

If you're klutzy, plan to distract him by giggling when you bonk noses. Smile wickedly at your prey when you happen to spill your mimosa all over the hors d'oeuvres as you run your hands through his hair. Act as if to say, *I meant to do that. Watch me now!* A sense of humor layered with a sense of erotic purpose and determination will make him forget all about the spilled drink—especially if you reveal a bit of cleavage when you mop it up. Then you get to say, as professionally and seriously as possible, "Now, where were we?"

Don't worry about your body image—it's all in the lips, the head, and the hips. You've got a sexy boy toy lined up as your erotic plaything: this situation won't be around forever, so make the most of what you've got to offer. Chances are, you're a lot sexier than you think—because sexy comes from inside, not outside. If you're worried about stacking up to others, in breast size or some other measurement, remember that bigger boobs won't make you sexier, they'll just make you someone with big boobs. Big breasts don't make you a hot kisser, either. And yes, men can say insensitive, critical, inappropriate things. If you find yourself making out with one of these clueless dudes, change the channel. Excuse yourself, and go make out with someone more worthy of your mad skills.

Build Tension

You'll start any make-out session with an appropriate choice of opening kisses: Chapter 2 tells you how to get started. Continue with an assortment of techniques described in chapter 4, including the Sweetheart Kiss, the Lusty Kiss, the Kama Sutra Kiss, Eskimo and Angel Kisses (starting out with no lips), or even the jump-him-now Mad Mack Attack Kiss. Then, once you've started that fire, turn up the heat by building erotic tension with your hands.

Move your hands to the part of your body where you want to focus his attention: the nape of the neck, eyes, lips, cleavage, or lower. Straighten your clothing (even though you know it's going to have to be straightened again), smooth your hair back, coyly replace a fallen bra strap. Or reach over and smooth out a wrinkle on his shirt or trousers.

Every once in a while, between kisses, touch yourself in ways that are suggestive, but never *too* outrageous. Naughty girl—you can even pretend your hands are his eyes. If you're seated, rub your calves or smooth your hands over your legs. Rub your hands over your arms almost as if you are cold, but slowly. Glide your hand across the back of your neck, feeling the softness of your skin, and even give it a momentary, gentle, stress-relieving rub. Rest your hands on your hips, or on your thighs.

Use your feet as well—feet are quite sexy. Take off a shoe and rub your ankle or foot. Or let one foot do a little recon, sneaking forward to touch his toe for a moment as if by accident, then back. Good feet, doing the dirty work. Then let one foot sneak up against his foot and apply a steady pressure, bringing his attention to the possibilities of both of your bodies touching. Gauge his reaction. See if he returns your pressure or moves away.

Accelerate His Attraction (without Giving Away Too Much)

A good speaker will stand so that his or her body is "open" to everyone listening, especially toward one person in particular. A make-out artist will do exactly the same while kissing. Have your feet apart, knees together (for now, anyway), and keep your arms open and uncrossed. Try to keep your head tilted down slightly to suggest directness in your kissing focus. Keep eye contact, but mix it up. You're one-on-one, so keep your eye contact consistent while kissing, but take 5-to-10-second visual breaks to let him look at you, too.

If he's primed for more and you want to know if you should turn up the heat, he'll give you signs and clues that are your green light. Unless he's really pawing on you or taking control, look for these "keep going" gestures: smiles, nods, little "mmh" noises that punctuate the breaks in your kisses, or small physical prompts like mirroring your kisses. He'll show increased attraction with his body (besides the, um, obvious) by leaning into you more, applying more pressure with his lips, and pulling you closer.

Give him what he wants—almost. And then a little bit more. You can direct his hands, which will likely be wandering. If he has them at the small of your back, slide them up your waist and to the sides of your breasts, all the while kissing, and then back to your waist. Turn down the heat with lighter kisses. Then bring his hands back near your breasts, and turn the heat back up with a hot, passionate kiss and a lower lip nibble. Now pull back for a smile.

Make-out Techniques: Light and Flirty or Down and Dirty

Review your quiz answers from chapter 1 to see what style of kissing vixen you are, and determine your course of make-out action based on how you scored. Let your inner Sweet Lips, Power Puss, Hot Lips, or Miss Pure Delicious Poison guide the way. Are you a little of each? No problem! Pick the ones you like to make a style all your own.

Sweet Lips Chic

Use your loveliest blossoms to attract the bees to your
honey: no matter how you want your kissing sessions to
go, your best technique depends on your smile, a knowing
look, and easy laughter. Make the most of your Sweet Lips
techniques by really working up the first-kiss tips. If you
identify with the sexy librarian type, the area where you
most need polish will be how to get started. You'll get the
best guidance from the "First Kiss Do's and Don'ts" in
chapter 2.

> *The attitude:* He melts in your mouth, not in your
> hands.
>
> *The techniques, in order:* First Kiss, Sweetheart
> Kiss, Angel and Eskimo Kisses, Romantic Kiss,
> Snuggle Bunny Kisses. Get your specifics from
> the "Appetizers" and "Dish of the Day" menus
> in chapter 5.
>
> *Ideal make-out conditions:* Light and sunny.
> Daytime picnics, beaches, private pretty vistas,
> romantic walks, sunsets.
>
> *Make-out checklist:* Lip gloss, rose-colored
> glasses.

Power Puss Vogue

Ready to strike the right pose, pucker up, and reel in your bohunk with sass? Power Girl, in this book you get the most from tips about eye contact, and seek out any kissing fix-its in sections on how to deal with guys who don't kiss as well as they look. You've got the power to pull in anyone you want. You can do what you want with them—be ready to decide whether to go all the way or not.

The attitude: Slippery when wet.

The techniques, in order: First Kiss, Kama Sutra Kisses, Taste of What's to Come, French Kiss, Romantic Kisses. Get your finer points from the "Appetizers," "Dish of the Day," and "Dessert" menus in chapter 5.

Ideal make-out conditions: Hot and steamy. Bars, clubs, parties (especially theme parties), after-hours bashes, and even on your doorstep as a Goodnight session.

Make-out checklist: A sexy scent (perfume, moisturizer, body butter) and tasty lip gloss.

Hot Lips Bombshell

Get ready, Bombshell, because when you kiss a boy, he's not going anywhere until you set him free. Delivering a powerful opening kiss is as easy for you as taking candy from a baby boy—and so is letting him know that *you're* the candy he needs. And you've got the smoldering gaze to back it up. Polish up your pout and make your kissing techniques shine by making the most of tips and tricks on what to do once you're in place and the conversation's flowing. You need the most help in focusing on hands, arms, legs, and feet, and using them to your best advantage.

> *The attitude:* Dangerous curves.
>
> *The techniques, in order:* Mad Mack Attack, Taste of What's to Come, Kama Sutra Kisses, French Kiss, Romantic Kisses, more French Kisses. Pick your pinpoint techniques mostly from the "Dish of the Day" and "Dessert" menus in chapter 5.
>
> *Ideal make-out conditions:* Heat wave, all the way. Anything that gets you close and personal is where you can work your magic: an intimate corner of a pub, a booth, in a corner at a wedding dinner, the interrogation room, the scene of the crime, private parties, dark movie theaters, museums, cocktail affairs, and boardroom affairs.

Make-out checklist: A compact mirror for lipstick fix-its when you need the pause that refreshes (or you get caught) and super-sexy underwear.

Miss Pure Delicious Poison

Men: they're what's for dinner. Style, panache, and a touch of supervillainess insanity make you the most magnetic and kissable woman in the room, whether you're arriving in an explosion of smoke, gliding in on the backs of your henchmen, or simply sitting on your mechanical throne stroking your fluffy white cat. Who cares if you come on too strong when you're the one holding the ray gun? Making men melt with your lips comes naturally; the only spot you need to perfect is the switch—when things don't go as planned, you get cranky. Don't seek vengeance—just keep your exit strategies in line. And don't forget that turning *down* the volume of your kissing powers can be just as powerful as cranking them up.

> ***The attitude:*** When I'm bad, I'm better.
> ***The techniques, in order:*** Mad Mack Attack, Lusty Kiss, Kama Sutra Kisses, French Kiss, reverse Gladiator Kisses, tease him down with

some Sweetheart Kisses, then come back with more French Kisses. Choose heavily from the "Dessert" menu in chapter 5.

Ideal make-out conditions: Your affections and your make-out sessions are like a storm. They rage in, wreak havoc, and subside just as quickly. Dramatic conditions suit you best: castles, underground labs, back rooms, rooftops, evil lairs, tech conferences, haunted woods, abandoned shacks, private islands, penthouse suites, ice fortresses, and secret hideouts.

Make-out checklist: Daytime disguise in your purse or utility belt, and edible body butter.

Wicked flirt checklist: Bad girl, good girl. It's an endless cycle. Now you're ready to join the party. Don't leave the house without your utility belt, magic lasso, and kick-ass bag of kissing tricks and techniques. Make notes and try to keep track of your conquests—kissing legends all have lists on their refrigerators, too.

Chapter 9

KISSING GAMES

Kissing is seductive, kissing is playful; but kissing is also a technique to be learned and refined like an artist, and a skill to be played like an athlete. A girl who is a make-out artist will go down in history as a legend whose kisses are talked about and compared to the finest paintings or the most erotic sculptures a guy would ever want to wrap his lips around. But if you really want to play the game like a skilled gambler, laying down a winning hand the moment you get to his table, I know you're ready if you've learned the techniques in this book. And when it comes to kissing games, I know you're going to play to *win*.

As of this writing, there is yet to be a Kissing Olympics, though every Valentine's Day around the world, various cities hold kissing contests. Power Puss alert: can you imagine finding the guy you'd kiss forever, and then showing the world you actually can? Well, in Nanning, China, there's a kissing contest in which one couple kissed for seven hours nonstop to win. But that's nothing compared to the Houston, Texas, couple who kissed for 22 hours straight in 2009: a bridal company organized the "Longest Kiss Contest" to win a dream wedding. Hopefully, the grand prize included a case of medical-grade ChapStick.

It's one thing to be primed to win a gold medal for kissing—that makes you a top player. It's another to have a roster of kissing games at your disposal, and to know which game would be most suitable in a particular situation, so you can walk away the smiling champ. There are games for two and games for groups. Now it's time to learn the games, and the rules of engagement. Even if you're already engaged.

Party Games

You've got the right attitude and the skills to pay the lip gloss bills; now it's time to show who's the Queen. At racy parties where there are a number of hotties out and about, the best way to break the ice is with a kissing game. You can play kissing games in large or small groups, in a room off to the side or in the middle of the show—for the maximum, delicious tension of seeing who's attracted to whom, and for the pleasure of showing off. Small parties or gatherings can turn entirely into a kissing game. Any way you do it, playing with a crowd of fun-loving, adventurous kissers is a blast. Achieve liftoff with the following kissing party games.

Spin the Bottle

Requirement: an empty bottle.

The most common kissing game in the world. A group of any size sits in a circle and people take turns spinning an empty bottle. The person spinning the bottle has to kiss whomever the bottle ends up pointing to; the group can self-determine if same-sex kissing is okay, or not—it's all in fun. Then the person who was kissed gets to spin the bottle to see whom she kisses next. Variations on this game include going in a circle to make sure everyone gets a turn and deciding whether the kissers do the deed in front of the group or run off to a closet or bathroom for the kiss.

Sixty Seconds in Heaven

Requirements: an empty bottle, a private space (closet), red lipstick, and a timer.

This is a classic, handed down through the ages by teenagers of all stripes. It's a great add-on to Spin the Bottle: The person who gets control of the bottle spins it twice and sends the random couple into a closet for 60 seconds. To increase the stakes, the pair must prove that they shared a kiss—with red lipstick. To play this game to win, one partner slathers their lips with the red lipstick and kisses the other as many times as possible on any area of exposed skin (face, neck, arms, etc.), leaving one lip print for each kiss. When the 60 seconds is up, the closet is opened and lip prints are counted. The pair who left the most lip prints wins. This game can also be played with pairs of already-established couples—each pair of love bunnies gets 60 seconds to kiss as much as possible and win the game.

Kissing Bunny

Requirements: a stuffed animal (like a bunny).

Sit in a circle and arrange yourselves either guy/girl or randomly; you'll be kissing whomever sits next to you. The stuffed bunny is the stunt bunny—the kissing double. One person takes the bunny and kisses it where they'd like to be kissed, then passes the bunny to the person on their right. The recipient has to kiss them on that spot. Then the person with the bunny kisses the bunny, passes it to the right, and gets their kiss, and so on. After one full circle, reverse the process and pass the bunny to the left. Variations: no part of the bunny can be kissed twice; or, for true gamblers, combine it with Spin the Bottle.

Pass the Apple

Requirements: a few apples.

A circular seating arrangement is best for this one as well, so arrange yourselves either guy/girl or randomly; you'll be kissing whomever sits next to you. One person takes an apple in their mouth and bites it, then passes it with their mouth to the person on their right. The recipient has to receive the apple using only their mouth, grabbing it with a bite. This will take some giggly coordination between the two of them. The apple will get smaller and smaller—until you need a new apple. After one full circle, reverse the process and pass the apple to the left.

Who's for Dessert?

Requirements: whipped cream, chocolate sauce, cherries, or any other lickable dessert topping that's handy.

This game can be played going around the circle or with the randomness of Spin the Bottle. The person who gets to receive the kiss takes the whipped cream or topping and places it where they'd like to have their "kiss." They can put it wherever they want, or you can set limits. The person who spun the bottle (or whoever's turn it is to do the kissing/licking) has to creatively kiss or nibble the dessert topping off.

The Mystery Kiss

Requirements: blindfolds, scarves, ties, or handkerchiefs.

Separate an even number of guys and girls (or however you want to mix it up) and stand across the room from each other, with the men blindfolded. Each girl selects a guy, quietly walks over and kisses him, making sure not to let him know who she is. Playing music will help hide any noise that might give your identity away. After each girl gives a guy a kiss, the ladies line up across the room from the men. The boys take off their blindfolds and try to guess who kissed them. If the boy guesses correctly, the girl is "out." The game continues until there is only one left. Next, swap blindfolds and the guys get their turn.

Games Just for Two

Are you ready to go one-on-one? A little hand-to-hand, or lips to—other places? Kissing games for two are a great way to melt the ice (literally, in one of these games) or spice up what might be an ordinary date, an evening around the house, or anytime you want to make the most of what's right in front of you.

Ice Princess

Requirement: a drink with ice cubes in it or a cup of ice.

Get an ice cube; start with it in your mouth, running it over his lips, his cheek and jaw, down his neck, or even his forearms and the sensitive hollow in the palm of his hand. Continue back up to his mouth and then it's his turn.

Ice, Ice, Baby (More)

Requirements: a drink with ice cubes in it or a cup of ice, and a timer.

Lay your victim down and place an ice cube on his stomach. Then have him gently sit up, allowing the ice cube to slide down his stomach. Wherever it lands, you have to lick and kiss for exactly one minute.

Chocolate Kisses

Requirements: fudge sauce or warmed chocolate syrup, and a spoon or paintbrush.

A delicious turn-on that lets you tease and tempt, or even draw or write messages on your lover's body. With a bottle of hot fudge or chocolate syrup in hand, have your partner lie down or lean back in a comfy chair. Take his shirt off (or pull it up) and draw or paint on a part of his body with the chocolate. Now lick and kiss it off.

Back to the Drawing Board

Requirements: lipstick and edible body paints (or colorful dessert topping).

Lightly draw lip prints someplace on your partner's exposed skin (lipstick or gourmet body paint works well for this). Then fill each of those marks with your own lips! This is especially fun with the body paints.

Blindfold Swap

Requirements: two blindfolds, scarves, ties, or handkerchiefs.

Both partners blindfold each other. Without using your hands, take turns giving exactly ten kisses to each other.

Catch Me If You Can

Tell him you want him to give you one kiss but you're not going to let him. When he tries to kiss your cheek, turn your head. If he aims for your lips, duck so he gets your nose. Spice it up by teasing him a little: when he's the one resisting your kisses, try to persuade him to give in and let you kiss him. This is a great game for a dating couple.

Queen of Hearts

Requirements: a deck of playing cards.

Remove all the hearts from a deck of ordinary playing cards. One of you shuffles the hearts, fans them out between you, and the other randomly chooses a card that decides how many kisses you will give. Variation: use dice and assign the following body parts to a six-sided die:

1: cheek

2: forehead

3: lips/mouth

4: neck

5: palm of the hand

6: anything goes

Not a Drinking Game

Requirement: a film that includes a repetitive activity that could be used for a typical "drinking game." Examples: watching *The Thin Man* and taking a drink every time the characters do; watching a Coen Brothers film and drinking every time an expletive (such as *f**k*) is used; whenever Buffy kills a vampire. You can even watch kissing movies, as recommended in chapter 7.

Whenever the repetitive activity (drinking, swearing, vampire slaying) happens onscreen, you and your partner kiss, but you can't touch each other in any other way until the movie is over.

Macho Man

Requirement: a guy who brags about how strong he is.

Does he think he's tough? Tough enough to get to kiss you? Challenge him to do a set of push-ups—where you make the rules. Lie flat on your back on the floor with your arms at your sides. His assignment is to "drop and give you twenty"—twenty kisses. He does push-ups over you, and every time he comes down he gets a reward: a kiss.

Stare Down

You and your partner have a staring contest; the goal is not to blink. The longer you keep your eyes open, the longer he gets to kiss you.

Hey, Driver: Stop Signs

While the two of you are driving, if you come to a stop sign that is a three- or four-way stop, the passenger has to kiss the driver that many times.

Anything for a Kiss

Here, almost anything goes: except kissing. The object of the game is to try to get him to kiss you by doing as you wish to him. You can do anything to lure him to your lips, but you cannot kiss him. Then switch, and he does the same to you. The person to last the longest without giving in wins.

Invisible Ink

With the tip of your tongue, spell a word on the upturned palm of his hand—or the inside of his forearm, his neck, or for the more adventurous, a place he can't see at all. If you want, spell out an instruction, such as "Kiss my right shoulder." If he gets it right, he either follows the instruction (which is its own reward) or gets to kiss you once anywhere he likes. If he gets it wrong, you get to do what you want to him. Take turns spelling words with your tongue.

The Magic Word

Each of you decides on a particular word at the beginning of the day, or on a day you have scheduled for a date, but don't tell each other what it is. Throughout the day (or during the date), if either of you says the other person's word, you have to drop everything and kiss the other person immediately.

ABOUT THE AUTHOR

VIOLET BLUE (tinynibbles.com) is a blogger, high-profile tech personality, award-winning best-selling author and editor of more than two dozen books in five languages, podcaster, reporter for Web TV show GETV, technology futurist, and sex-positive pundit in mainstream media such as CNN and *The Tyra Banks Show*. She is the sex columnist for the *San Francisco Chronicle*, with a weekly column titled "Open Source Sex," and she runs a podcast by the same name with more than 8 million downloads and counting. Violet is also a *Forbes* Web Celeb and one of *Wired*'s Faces of Innovation. She writes for media outlets such as *Forbes*; *O, The Oprah Magazine*; and the UN-sponsored international health organization RH Reality Check.

Violet gives lectures to cyberlaw classes at UC Berkeley, human sexuality programs at UCSF, and tech conferences (ETech and SXSW), in addition to sex crisis counselors at community teaching institutions and Google Tech Talks. Her tech blog is at techyum.com, and she publishes DRM-free audio and e-books at DigitaPub.com.